GLORIOUS
GARDENS

GLORIOUS
GARDENS

With a Commentary by Francesca Greenoak

Conran Octopus

First published in 1989 by
Conran Octopus Limited
37 Shelton Street
London WC2H 9HN

Reprinted 1990

Project Editor	Lorraine Dickey
Editor	Catherine Carpenter
Art Director	Mary Evans
Designer	Mike Snell
Picture Research	Nadine Bazar
Production	Michel Blake and Jackie Kernaghan
Botanists	Timothy Walker and Sarah Bradshaw
Editorial Assistant	Elizabeth Brooks

British Library Cataloguing in Publication Data
Greenoak, Francesca
  Glorious gardens: a portfolio of ideas for planting
  and design.
  1. Gardens. Landscape design. Amateurs'
  I. Title
  712'.6

ISBN 1-85029-205-1

Typeset by MS Filmsetting Limited, Frome, Somerset
Printed in Hong Kong

CONTENTS

INTRODUCTION

What we grow in our gardens is quite as much an expression of personal taste as the way we furnish our living rooms: whether we choose to have lilies, hollyhocks and columbines by the pathsides or prim, beautifully kept topiary. Yet gardening is more than an exercise in exterior decoration because it involves not inanimate objects but a living environment. Even in the tiniest back yard, one is involved in a relationship with the earth itself.

This book is about plants and the ways in which people grow them in their gardens. Looking through these pictures, it strikes me forcibly that the gardens consist not principally of plants of extreme rarity and difficulty but more often ones which are really rather easily grown and commonly available. Success lies not so much in professional services and expense as in individual creativity and experimentation.

Seeing the things other gardeners have achieved can often spark off new ideas for one's own garden. This book is an armchair introduction, a directory of ideas for plant associations and individual effects. It consists of thematic sections, each exploring the possibilities of a specific style of gardening. This may be dictated by the nature of the site or by personal taste. The ideas explored are drawn from all over the world, and, although arranged separately, are not in practice exclusive. One could try a number of themes within one garden.

Although this book is primarily a guide to ideas rather than a manual, I do consider it important to select good forms of garden plants (something a beginner can easily overlook) so wherever it has been possible I have given the full names of select varieties or cultivated forms. This can sometimes be a bit off-putting when it involves scientific Latin and a complicated following name but it is well worth making the extra effort to find the right plant.

Lavender 'Hidcote', for example, is much neater and more compact than the rather leggy common lavender, and much the best choice if you want it for an edging or tightly packed lavender bed, whereas the catnip 'Six Hills Giant' is extremely generous in its flowering and can be depended upon for a good show of purple misty flowers right through late summer and into autumn. Discovering such plants among the general mêlée and finding ways of planting them to best effect is one of the great joys of the garden.

A view to the countryside at Fontainebleau through an archway of vines and roses. The climbing white 'Seagull', 'Kiftsgate', 'Wedding Day', 'Rambling Rector' and 'Bobby Jones' grow with pale lush 'Félicité et Perpétue', pink 'New Dawn' and 'Pink Cloud'.

THE
WALLED GARDEN

A wall can itself be a thing of beauty, which may seem obvious, but it is something to consider before planning a hanging smother of evergreen. Few things can beat the combination of a climbing plant, such as clematis, jasmine or rose, skillfully trained on a good wall, the colours and textures of wall, foliage and flowers intermingling. Deciduous climbers or wall-trained fruit provide a continuously changing drama through the seasons. Even in the long months of winter they are beautiful in their own way, with a display of grey or brown bark and red and purple buds against stone or pale brick.

Wisteria, roses and honeysuckle are traditional choices for walls, and clothe them beautifully, but many other plants are available. The Virginia creeper preferred by the French (also known as Boston ivy), *Parthenocissus tricuspidata*, which has three-lobed leaves, goes redder and seems to hold its colour longer than the more rampant *P. quinquefolia*, with five serrated leaflets, which has a brilliant but short-lived autumn glory. Vines such as the dainty (and edible) variety of the grape vine called 'Brandt' and the ornamental *Vitis coignetiae* also give splendid autumn colour, which is often the more striking when in the drier, poorer soil near a wall.

One of the benefits of gardening on sunny and warm walls is that they will shelter and support somewhat tender plants which could not otherwise be grown. The pretty but rather delicate fremontodendron, with nice foliage and yellow flowers, and the winter-flowering chimonanthus both like the extra warmth and protection of a wall. In mild climates the lacy pink nerines and similarly tender plants enjoy the beds at the base of walls. 'Plumbago' *Ceratostigma willmottianum* thrives in wall crevices, providing rich blue flowers into the autumn when its foliage begins to redden as the weather cools.

Even dark cold walls can be called to good account, with fruit such as morello cherry and 'Victoria' plum, or the delightful *Hydrangea petiolaris* with its lace-edged flowers in the summer and glossy cinnamon twigs in the winter. *Garrya elliptica*, a California evergreen, notable for the greyish tassel-like catkins of the male plant, likes a sheltered shady position, but is susceptible to cold, chilling winds.

A quiet blue-grey corner with rich, orange-red narrow
trumpet flowers of the semi-evergreen honeysuckle
(*Lonicera sempervirens*) being trained up the wall. The rose is
'Breeze Hill' (usually more orange-pink). The fast-growing
Canary Island ivy (evergreen except in hard winters)
provides a glossy background for the sink gardens.

TOP LEFT These walls, built in local sandstone, provide a 2 m (6½ ft) high shelter for the plants within this garden on the edge of moorland. Eighteenth-century stone vases holding ground ivy stand at the entrance. Within may be glimpsed an island of colourful plants, the golds and reds brightest against the dark stone and green foliage.

The rich allium flowerheads are eye-catching in bright pink and deep crimson (probably *Allium aflatuense* and its near relative, the variety 'Purple Sensation'). The red poppy is another beacon (not the field poppy but a variety of the taller *Papaver orientale*). It is significant that, within a cold windswept region, plants in this sheltered garden are undamaged –

though few grow higher than the surrounding walls.

ABOVE LEFT This wall forms part of the outer wall of a dry garden within the larger design of Athelhampton in Dorset. In the fairly mild climate of southern England, the subtropical plants of this garden are further protected by the walls. Mounted in

the alcove is a lion's head fountain, which spurts water into the urn beneath. This in turn overflows into the lead basin, which overflows into the semicircular pond. The upper planting is beautiful Arum lilies (*Zantedeschia*), which are white when in flower and have a lovely glossy foliage. The lower planting is both pink and white water liles.

ABOVE A walled, paved section of garden in cool colours. The Coalbrookdale bench with its complicated fern-leaf motif as a classic of nineteenth-century design in cast iron; it is sheltered by a fragrant arbour of 'Constance Spry' rose, while the useful white hydrangea (*Hydrangea petiolaris*), which grows well in shade, climbs the adjacent

wall. This hydrangea is self clinging but it does better with a little help. Four shapely terracotta pots of box give a formal flavour, softened by informal clumps of cottage garden plants in blues, pinks and mauves, such as foxglove, delphinium, monkshood (aconite), geranium and campanula, with *Stachys* and paeony adding silver and white.

ABOVE A high drystone wall of Cotswold limestone plays host to a range of common lime-loving plants, making a bright cushion capping the well-built, traditional wall.

As the daffodils and narcissi of the upper lawn begin to fade, pink and crimson aubrieta varieties, the yellow alyssum (*Alyssum saxatile*), pinky-red islands of saxifrage, arabis and feather-leaved, silver-grey cineraria or dusty miller (*Senecio bicolor cineraria*) begin their flowering season.

As yet, this is a young, raw wall; within a few years, these plants and others, such as ivy-leaved toadflax, yellow corydalis and wall ferns, will have colonized the interstices between the neat dry-stone knaps. Oddly, self-seeding on walls is usually surer than planting seeds or plantlets into compost-filled crevices.

RIGHT Wall decoration in layers: a border with a low-growing blue-green euphorbia with lime-green flowerheads (probably *Euphorbia cyparissias*) backed by a bed of taller pinky-mauve which is *Erysimum* 'Bowles Mauve'. This is a plant very similar in appearance to wallflower, with a slight scent and blue-grey foliage. It is perennial but tends to become leggy with age.

A dense yew hedge overhangs the wall making an umbrella for the rose below. The full blooms of warm apricot-buff tones identify it as 'Gloire de Dijon', a rose which does not do well in the wet, though it needs light and sun, and enjoys the warm shelter afforded by a wall. The stems of climbing roses need to be tied on to nails or pegs discreetly (but securely) fixed into the wall.

LEFT The violet colour of the clematis clothing the inner corner of this garden is taken up by the pansies at ground level, while the lavender mediates softly within the same colour spectrum.

Clematis × jackmanii, with purple blooms and green stamens, is one of the best known of all clematis varieties. There is also a form called *C. × jackmanii* 'Superba', even darker and richer in colour, while the variety 'H. F. Young' has wide, well-shaped petals with creamy stamens. Attractive walls such as this one should not be smothered in plants.

ABOVE A brick alcove covered in wisteria, with a *trompe d'oeil* effect created by a backdrop of the golden ivy 'Buttercup'. Wisteria is an excellent and popular choice for training on large pergolas and walls, which it covers vigorously and quickly. This one is the double form *Wisteria sinensis* 'Plena' (there is also a white form, 'Alba'). To bloom its best, wisteria needs a sunny wall and careful pruning. Ivy is self-clinging, so it needs no supports but it can be made to grow in one direction or another and pruned (cut not pulled) when necessary.

RIGHT The leaves of this decorative vine (*Vitis coignetiae*) tend to turn to more brilliant autumn colours when it is planted in dry, somewhat poor soil, such as one often finds at the base of a wall. Sometimes called the Japanese crimson glory vine, it is best in a large garden where it has plenty of room to spread and display its autumn colour.

It grows extremely fast and vigorously, rising to a robust 22–36 m (75–100 ft) given a large building or tree for support. On a wall it needs training and pruning when it has reached the required height and spread (shoots should be cut back to a point above a healthy-looking bud). In late summer old or dying branches should be removed and young shoots can be shortened.

This is a plant which likes chalky or high-lime soil and dolomite lime should be added to acid soil where *Vitis coignetiae* is to be grown. It will grow most vigorously in soil which is composted, manured and deeply dug, but may be slow to colour in these ideal conditions.

This vine is growing on a house with a narrow border, mostly containing herbs at its foot.

BELOW RIGHT A large, spreading, wall-trained actinidia (*Actinidia kolomikta*) grown for its extremely decorative foliage. It is luxuriantly bushy in growth and each of its heart-shaped dark green leaves merges into pink or white or a blend of both colours towards the tip.

This actinidia will grow to 3.75 m (10–12 ft) in height on a sheltered warm wall with a greater spread. In its early days it will need careful tying-in to supports. Cats seem to be especially attracted to this species and there are many stories of damage or death caused to young bushes by cats, so some form of guard is a good idea until the plant gets well established.

It is a shrub grown for foliage effect. It has midsummer flowers, which are small, white and roundish. Male and female flowers are usually on separate plants, and a pair may produce viable seed which can be sown in autumn. Actinidia can also be propagated by cuttings, taken in late summer and grown in a sandy compost in a propagator until they have taken root. Actinidias will not thrive on soil with a high lime content; they like a richly organic, well-drained loam and will do well in sun or semi-shade.

BELOW FAR RIGHT A *Clianthus* (parrot's bill) this size is something of a triumph and can only be attempted in places with mild winters, where the plant can have a sheltered wall, preferably one against which it can show its brilliant colour to best effect.

Its attractive foliage has a feathery appearance because each of the long leaves is composed of numerous leaflets. Clusters of flowers, like deep red claws, appear in early summer on plants over three years old. There are also pink and white forms.

This kind of *Clianthus* can be grown indoors in a conservatory (sun porch) or greenhouse in cold areas, providing the temperature does not stay below 5°C (41°F), and the plant is kept moist to deter red spider mite. Out of doors, the roots should be well blanketed with peat covered with bracken, and in hard frosts, hanging mats over the branches (as they did in the old walled gardens) will help prevent damage.

THE
ANNUAL GARDEN

Annual garden plants, most of them from hot countries which have harder, more brightly coloured plants than natives to northern countries, were all-pervasive in the gardens of just over a century ago. The fashion for 'carpet bedding' with annuals became discredited over the years, largely owing to the influence of gardeners such as Bowles, Robinson and Gertrude Jekyll, who favoured a more 'natural appearance', and held that the time and labour expended on the brightly patterned arrangements were out of proportion to the results.

Miss Jekyll, however, was not so extreme as to dismiss all annual plants. She rejoiced in their brightness when they were planted for individual character, not merely as part of a geometric pattern. She loved geraniums in pots, and admired the scarlet salvias which are popular to this day.

Annual bedding plants are still an important element of gardening, although the passion for spectacular carpet bedding is limited to splendidly gaudy private gardens, municipal gardens and floral set-pieces comme-morating local festivals and events. In these areas there are some imaginative modifications: the planting of the Barbican Centre in London, for example, uses lemon-yellow broom with wallflowers, or euphorbias underplanted with tulips, in displays which create a most welcome lightness in an architecturally grey and overwhelming environment.

Fashion swings one way and another. Some present-day gardeners are still as devoted to growing annual flowers as ever, but they tend to use them in different ways, planting them among the perennial plants, dotting the garden with patches of bright colour.

French marigolds, red salvias, alyssum and lobelia, and especially petunias, are still sold in huge numbers as seeds and plantlets. Nemesias, pelargoniums (geraniums) and named varieties of poppy are also popular. Many of these are not truly annuals in the botanical sense but are simply not up to the harshness of a cool climate; in their own lands, the species from which these garden cultivars are bred would flower year after year under a bright sun. Borrowed from their native climes, these bold, indiscreet plants add a unique element of drama and who – amongst even the most conservatively subtle gardeners – would deny the pleasure of sweet peas, larkspur, stocks, antirrhinums (snapdragons) or love-in-a-mist?

Bright, fragrant wallflowers, so much appreciated in early spring, are actually perennials, but treated as biennials by gardeners who grow them from seed and as annuals by those who buy plants from garden centres in autumn to flower a few months later, after which they will be removed to make way for the next display.

ABOVE A two-tone border in a garden in France which stars the French marigold *Tagetes patula* (which, confusingly, the French call *oeillet d'Inde* or carnation of the Indies). These frilled orange and crimson flowers, which look slightly carnation-like in their double form, are among the most popular annual plants, not perhaps to everybody's taste, but undeniably striking, particularly when grown with the narrow, dark blue-purple flower spikes of *Salvia × superba*.

Tall, lily-like agapanthus rise above the salvias, but it is undoubtedly the combination of the marigold and violet which makes the main drama.

French marigolds grow wild in Mexico and were imported to Europe in the sixteenth century; they were then (reputedly) taken to England by Huguenot refugees, producing their first blooms in 1572. By the mid-1700s this species was pronounced by gardener John Hill to be almost 'more common in gardens than the Polyanthus', another great favourite.

French marigolds are tolerant of most soils, but do best in a rich, fertile medium. Seeds sown under glass in March or April will have grown rapidly enough to be planted outside

in May and will flower reliably all summer long. They come in single and double varieties in lemon, orange and crimson single colours and combinations.

Salvia × superba is a perennial plant which makes a valuable contribution to the garden, as a foil to annuals as here, or in company with flowering shrubs such as roses or other herbaceous perennials.

ABOVE A muddle of colours which should clash but mix excitingly in a flowerbed. Eschscholzia, or Californian poppies, are bright orange in their native lands, but have been bred to produce pinks and red, crimson, orange, gold and cream. There are varieties which have an increased number of petals, making some of the flowers almost double, but some of the fragile beauty of their form is lost

in the doubling. It is still possible to buy single eschscholzias, either in single or mixed colours.

The plant in the foreground is Venus's looking glass (Specularia speculum-veneris). Echium lycopsis makes a quiet background of blue-purple for the lively eschscholzias. All of these plants thrive in light soils on sunny sites and can be grown successfully in situ in spring.

LEFT The symmetry of pots filled with mauve violas makes all the difference to the entrance of a house in classical style. The hedge is evergreen euonymus, the neat climbers two kinds of Virginia creeper: flowers and colours are confined to the container plants, and here the owner has eschewed the idea of a potpourri of different plants and mixed colours, opting for a subtle, clear statement in a pastel colour. Containers are often at their most effective when used in this way. The range of violas available to the gardener is huge, including some which can be used in outdoor pots during the winter.

ABOVE An old stone trough makes an ample and unusual container for a delightful display of annuals. Pinks and purples look best against grey stone and a variety of plants in this colour range has been densely planted with the grey-white *Helichrysum petiolare* arching down at each end to white pelargoniums (geraniums).

There are only a few types of plants in the large trough – petunias, pelargoniums and lobelia – but since they are in a variety of shades, the effect is busy without being fussy. The small lobelia (*Lobelia erinus*) has a pretty flower which can only be properly admired if it is grown in a raised container.

TOP Annuals blooming against a background of fastigiate Irish yew in southern England in early September. The cosmea make a pretty show of pinks amongst a haze of light green foliage. These are garden forms of the Mexican plant *Cosmos bipinnatus*. Sown in February under glass, they will begin flowering in August and in a hot dry season present quantities of flower until the first frosts. The sweet peas behind need a richer soil but if the faded blooms are continually removed they will give a long display of sweetly scented blooms.

ABOVE A sight to warm a seed-merchant's heart: a sea of annuals in waves of colour, all grown from seed by the owner. The sweet peas, supported by strings and poles, make a screen, in front of which sweeps a line of larkspur in colours from blue-white to purple. Other plants include mauve to purple claries, marigolds, nasturtiums, godetias and stocks tangled together in colourful turbulence, making a pretty cottage-garden effect, while a tall curtain of runner beans adds its scarlet flowers to the general effect.

The sweet pea, one of the most popular annual species, has the unusual benefit of beauty in both appearance and scent (although it must be said that some of the boldly coloured modern varieties have only a slight fragrance compared with their old-fashioned counterparts). Fortunately, many seed firms have realized that the distinctive sweet-pea fragrance is part of its appeal and have brought back into their catalogues some of the most fragrant of the old varieties and are also breeding new hybrids from them.

One of the problems of sweet-pea growing is that the long-legged, easily damaged stems require support and this is rarely an asset within a garden design. This clump of sweet pea 'Quito' at the Royal Horticultural Society's gardens at Wisley in Surrey, England, is an honourable exception. The sweet-pea stems are woven in and out of an elegant trellis which looks as if it might be attached to a balustrade. There can hardly be a nicer way to decorate a screen dividing one piece of garden from the next than with scented flowers.

THE
WATER GARDEN

Water, basic to life, is almost as vital to garden design. Those gardens which look out to the sea, or are bounded by a river or have a small stream running through them have an incomparable natural asset. Trying to imitate or even improve on the effects of nature, landscapers of past and present have contrived diverse and ingenious water effects, from the huge, elaborate fountains of the great gardens of Europe to artificial lakes and the glassy, contained effects of formal pools, reflecting traditional or modern sculpture.

Water in a smaller modern garden challenges the ingenuity of domestic gardeners and professional landscapers alike. In general the smaller the space, the more restrained and delicate the use of water has to be. A popular option is a tiny spout, mounted on a wall, while a slightly more ambitious scheme involves a stone- or brick-edged raised pool which can capture the sound of water by use of a trickling rivulet which is channelled down an open half-pipe to fall into the pool. The purpose of these effects is to bring the sound of water into the garden and the smallest pumps must be used to achieve such a gentle flow. A small lion's head spout with the most delicate trickle of water, set within the pleasant flowery greenery of a tiny town garden, can completely distract one from the roar of traffic, though the busiest of roads may be only a matter of feet away.

Still water designed on a grand scale to mirror summerhouses, sculpture, superb trees or classical temples has been the model for smaller gardens, where one of these features can be employed for a single, elegant effect. Plants growing in, and beside, still waters impede reflection, but can be an art form in themselves whether you opt for native wild plants or exotic flora. In a garden of half an acre or so, it is possible to create a naturalistic pond (butyl-lined), graduated in depth with soft-edged grassy sides, which will support waterplants and attract a wealth of wildlife. Grading the shallows into a small marshy patch also gives a good habitat for damp-loving plants such as mimulus, sweet flag, globe flower, *Houttuynia* with leaves which have an odour of bitter oranges and the sulphur-yellow Himalayan primula. If you have room, butterbur (*Petasites* spp.) and gunnera with their huge leaves provide drama and glamour.

The owner of this garden decided upon a raised pool so the surround could act as a low seat from which to enjoy the sound and feel of the water, and the flowers – water lilies (the cultivar 'James Brydon'), irises and purple loosestrife. The pretty rose 'Clair Matin' flowers all summer through, toning with the blues and pinks of the brick.

LEFT The brick-edged raised pool echoes the shape of the box-edged flowerbeds, giving a formal structure within the garden which accommodates generous planting.

Roses and foliage within the flowerbed break the geometrical line, while around the pool, terracotta pots of flowers perform the same function, and the large water lily leaves thrust themselves up the sides. Around the edge of the garden, catnip and tall, spreading shrub roses flower in happy abandon against curtains of ash and ivy foliage.

ABOVE This softly planted pool used to be a drinking pond for the farm animals. The sandy-grey coloured drystone embankments and walls make a good medium both to grow and show the plants.

Alchemilla mollis, forget-me-nots, candytuft, rockrose and Jacob's ladder grow informally between the stones, while tall spear-like irises and ferns rise taller. Different levels around the pool make a scene like a graduated rock garden, with the terracotta amphora and jar serving as stylish and shapely ornaments.

ABOVE People with very small
gardens or very small children have
discovered that a fountain over rock
or stones (as top left) makes an
attractive, compact and safe means of
enjoying water in the garden. An
enclosing circle of box gives a chic
finishing touch. It also hides the edges
of the container which collects and
recycles the water via a small pump.
The plants growing outside the magic
circle are evidently prospering –
they are enjoying the double benefit
of the humidity and damp provided
by the fountain.

The simple effect of a pool
surrounded solely with a glossy-
leaved bergenia draws attention to the
detail of the fountain (top right) and
the sound of the water.

A half barrel can be used for water
plants (above left). This white water-
lily looks extremely healthy, but will
have to be severely pruned before it
becomes too congested. Early spring
is the best time to lift the root
container, cut off a strong-looking
rhizome with a sharp knife about a
hand's length down from the
growing part, trim its roots and

replant. Several miniature hybrids
suitable for small ponds or tubs are
now available.

A touch of imagination can create
an interesting scene by the simplest
means (above right). A shallow dish
has large stones arranged as a
surround and some refreshingly
unusual planting. Hoary plantain
(*Plantago media*) has pretty powder-
pink flowerheads and a rosette of soft
leaves, but is rarely used in gardens.
Grasses, moss and small alpine
alchemillas also form part of this
charming and distinctive display.

THE WATER GARDEN

ABOVE A still, calm scene with a ground-level pool reflecting sky and foliage. This is a garden which repays attention since it is closely planted with an interesting selection of foliage and flowering plants, most of which are shade-tolerant.

The plant with spear-like leaves on the left is a white *Tradescantia* × *andersoniana*. Two white forms are 'Innocence', which is pure white, and 'Osprey', which is white with blue centres. The flowers are unusual in that they are three-petalled. Its neighbour is an epimedium, a plant which is grown as much for its elegant leaves as its delicate sprays of tiny flowers. They do well in shade, thriving in damp, rich conditions. *Epimedium* × *rubrum* and *E. grandiflorum* 'White Queen' are good low-growing kinds while *E.* × *youngianum* 'Niveum' hangs its white flowers above chocolate-coloured foliage.

The blue-leaved herb rue is pretty but can cause problems to people with sensitive skin, so should be handled with respect (and gloves). This is especially important when taking cuttings or pruning. Growing beside it is one of the few plants with nearly black flowers: *Geranium phaeum*, also known as mourning widow. It is hardy and shade-tolerant, but should be bought in flower as there are colour forms which are less dark.

On the far side of the pool, the silver-green leaves of *Ballota pseudodictamnus* rise through another geranium. Near it is an interesting small, white-flowered campion and what looks like an old-fashioned chimney bellflower, *Campanula pyramidalis*, just about to flower.

31

LEFT A Dutch water garden with a substantial rectangular pool on two levels. The trailing plant, creeping Jenny, smothers a substantial part of the banks in light green foliage and starry yellow flowers. A magnificent group of hostas shows that the gardener appreciates them as flowering as well as foliage plants.

A new boardwalk has been made to join the older weathered one. Pink foxgloves, plumed astilbes and tall bamboos brighten the bank to the left of the picture.

The huge leaves of gunnera make great umbrellas at the end of the garden, while a tall gold-yellow flowered mullein leans swaying over the water.

ABOVE A pensive cherub presides over this tiny nook in a leafy corner of a small garden in Oxford, England. A scalloped dish catches rainwater, reflecting the shady greens which surround it.

The foliage from a large number of plants intermingles in a tumble of golds, greens, reds and creams. Box, fern and ivy in golden forms create a bright effect, tempered by the white lamium, columbine and red-tinged epimedium. A small bamboo and glossy arching foliage (Solomon's seal or the more unusual yellow *Uvularia*) overhang the statue, giving a sense of secrecy.

ABOVE A sunken water garden in the south-east of England in lush green early-summer freshness. The large leaves of gunnera and American skunk cabbage (*Lysichiton americanum*) dwarf the statue, while the tall stems of the candelabra primrose (*Primula bulleyana*) with their tiers of bright flowers rise tall in front of it. The graceful fronds of the beautiful ostrich fern and the spear-like leaves of the irises offer more variety in foliage, shape and texture.

At the far end of the pool, behind the large grasses and yellow loosestrife, a gap in the vegetation affords a view of steps rising to a clipped lawn, a distinct contrast to the lushness below. As autumn nears, the focus of this water garden will change as the eye is drawn upward to the changing colour of the swamp cypress, cotinus and maple which overhang the pool.

RIGHT This house and garden are appropriately named after the brook which meanders prettily through the garden. The waterside is edged with flowers and foliage in dappled shade under the trees, with the flowers taking the dominant role.

We look through columbines with astilbes to our left, down to the water course marked out by cheery mimulus, tall pale-pink valerian and an exotic group of candelabra primroses. Groups of plants cleverly echo each other on opposite sides of the brook as it winds its way around the garden, its curves followed by a sinuous gravel path.

A clump of *Iris sibirica* flowering richly makes a rich dark-blue focus, and, in the shade beyond, the Himalayan blue poppy (*Meconopsis betonicifolia*) blooms an unlikely deep sky-blue against the homely green English meadow which rises beyond.

THE
WINTER GARDEN

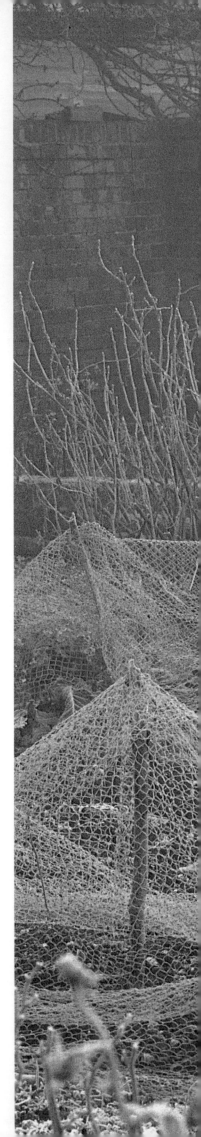

The garden in winter can be a joyful place. Imagine catching the scent of winter honeysuckle *Lonicera fragrantissima*, stronger for its seasonal unexpectedness; drinking in the softer scent of viburnum blooms bunched on the bare twigs and branches; or later enjoying the rich perfume of the pink flowers of the *Daphne mezereum*, a plant which does well in gardens though, alas, increasingly rare in British woodlands.

Winter flowers are especially valued because of their rarity. Colour is provided continuously by evergreens: box, yew, spiky butcher's broom or low-growing bronze-leaved gaultheria. Hardy ivies, such as the glossy Irish ivy, or pretty small-leaved ivies, such as the white-edged 'Glacier' or the ripple-leaved 'Green Ripple', are content to lurk recessively during the summer but make an important and elegant contribution to winter walls, fences and trees.

Coloured stems can be used to good effect, the most brilliant being those of the dogwoods. The best of the red-stemmed varieties is the startling *Cornus alba* 'Sibirica' and the best of the yellow-stemmed is *Cornus stolonifera* 'Flaviramea'.

When the lingering wintry months of the year stretch bleakly and apparently interminably, the early bulbs raise their heads – snowdrops, winter aconites and small irises – accompanied by braver perennials such as the lungworts, great cupped, pink-veined hellebores and the small, dainty pink *Corydalis solida*.

Most important in the winter garden is an overall design which can rest within the summer garden, revealing its own shape and form after the annuals have been removed and the perennials have died back into the ground. Deciduous trees and shrubs are an important but sometimes disregarded part of this pattern. A stark context shows up the textures and colours of bark: paperbark maples (*Acer griseum*), the flaking map-like *Betula ermanii*, the mahogany ribbons of *Prunus serrula*, the amber of *Prunus maackii* and gleaming birches with brown, white and silvery trunks. There are few sights more lovely than frost-laced boughs and twigs, or the individual colours and patterns of the buds and twigs of different trees, every bit as beautiful in their way as the fresh leaves of springtime.

Winter in a walled kitchen garden showing how exquisite a
well laid out garden can be during a time of year when it is
usually ignored. The light crusting of frost endows the
leaves of overwintering broccoli and even the netting with
a fairytale beauty, the brown stems of the black currants
catching the pale light of the low winter sun.

LEFT An armillary sphere reflects the sun on this crisp wintry day in the Netherlands, snowy snakes of box hedging losing definition under their blanket of snow.

TOP A garden under a light dusting of snow retains recognizable shapes, though the box balls look rather like Christmas puddings. The hydrangeas in pots retain their old flowerheads and should survive the winter so long as temperatures do not descend too far below zero for a long period, when they should be given some insulation or shelter (4°F or −15°C is the critical point). Plants grown in open ground will usually survive short periods at lower temperatures, though cold winds will damage foliage.

ABOVE LEFT Evergreen foliage in winter is bewitching. When there are fewer distractions in the garden, the character of colour and veining ornamented with frost can be thoroughly appreciated. *Cotoneaster salicifolius* 'Gnom' displays its ruddy stems and narrow leaves with the distinctive central vein.

ABOVE RIGHT One of the true glories of winter, common ivy takes a purplish tinge, its beautiful leaf shapes and branched veining revealed with great clarity.

ABOVE Gardens such as this are as crisply desirable on a cold winter's day as ever they are in the summer. A variegated holly, 'Golden King', clipped into two comfortably rounded tiers, dominates the foreground; the red of *Cotinus coggygria purpureus* flames beyond the burnished beech hedge. The bright scarlet hips of the *Rosa rugosa* gleam sparsely through its yellowing leaves, its foliage interwined with a clematis grown through it, with beautiful grey-white feathery seedheads. This must surely be *Clematis tangutica*, a late-flowering yellow-gold species which keeps its soft fluffiness well into the winter months.

RIGHT There is far more variety in a beech hedge than any evergreen could give; it changes from the palest, most delicate of greens in the spring to dark green and finally to a rich winter brown. If the hedge is given its final trim of the season quite early, about the last week in August, the leaves tend to hold on better, sometimes lasting throughout the winter. Beech can reach a height of about 3.5 m (10 ft) in five to six years, but even when immature, like this double hedge, it looks attractive. As it grows this hedge will make a kind of foliage 'house' at the end of the grass path, with the terracotta pot on the wall serving as its chimney.

ABOVE The glowing stems, dark evergreens, variegated foliage and precocious blooms draw visitors on the coldest days to the winter garden within the Cambridge Botanic Garden in England.

In the foreground is a clump of glowing red stems of *Cornus alba* 'Sibirica', underplanted with the low-growing *Euonymus fortunei* 'Silver

Queen'. Another group of crimson stems situated beyond is interspersed with clumps of a yellow-stemmed cultivar which is called *Cornus stolonifera* 'Flaviramea'.

The two reddish-stemmed shrubs, speckled with pale pink, to the right of the picture are *Viburnum* × *bodnantense* 'Dawn', which has early fragrant flowers that appear before the

leaves. To the left of the viburnums is the shining mahogany-coloured stem of a *Prunus rufa*, which was collected on a botanical trip to China and donated to the garden. (It is now available in nurseries.)

A bank of evergreen berberis rises up on the far side of the path and box clipped into low pyramids contributes texture to the scene.

TOP RIGHT It is during the winter months when structural and decorative elements often show to their best advantage, uncluttered by a dressing of luxuriant flowers and foliage. Shapely evergreens (clipped or unclipped), such as yew, box and ivy, are especially valuable.

Man-made structures also come into their own – winter gives a clear focus to statues, walls and gates. Fences (which can be draped with climbers) and gates, made in wrought iron, are particularly valuable artefacts in a garden design, giving a patterned window into another part of the garden landscape.

ABOVE RIGHT The tousled face of early winter closing in on autumn: bright, damp and cold. The sentinel yews (discreetly wired to maintain their close, dense shape) contrast with the grey of santolina (cotton lavender) bushes at their foot. Errant sprays of cotoneaster slide their horizontal stems between the lined yews, sunlight playing on the small, glossy leaves. All these plants keep their leaves throughout winter.

ABOVE Guelder rose is one of the most beautiful shrubs – a delight from its first pointed glossy leaves to its glistening red berries (top left).

It is a shame to cut back old seed-heads and stems when they look so attractive in the clear winter light. The dainty mops (above left) are stems of the giant cowslip *Primula florindae*, and the 'silver pennies' above the snowdrops (top right) are the seed heads of honesty. Plumed pampas grass (above right) bends over the ghostly white stems of an ornamental rubus (probably *Rubus biflorus*).

RIGHT Two of the nicest flowers of late winter and early spring are shown growing in a garden in the south of England. The beautiful pink and green cups of *Helleborus orientalis* begin to flower early and last for weeks and weeks. Named cultivars are very expensive but desirable forms create themselves in a fertile garden, self-seeding readily. The resulting flowers vary in size and colour from crimson-pink through to green. The small, bright daffodils are an especially early and attractive variety known as 'Tête-à-tête'.

THE
KITCHEN GARDEN

One of the most significant aspects of horticultural development in the late twentieth century is the return of the kitchen garden as an ornamental as well as productive part of gardening. The restoration of the remarkable *potager* at Villandry, in France, with its formal pattern of beautifully planted vegetable beds, has been an inspiration to many gardeners. In England Rosemary Verey has made her own version of the *potager* within her Gloucestershire garden at Barnsley House. It has a geometrical framework, plotted out by narrow paths made of the distinctive bricks and stones which she has collected. In the beds are clusters of rose bushes and festooned fruit trees, and colourful, richly textured vegetable plantings. It is striking, fragrant and full of wit: a triangular onion bed adjoins a plot of red-stemmed Swiss chard and is decorated with oak-leaf lettuce; a tunnel combines sweet peas and vegetable marrows.

In recent times, there has been a return to the 'cottage garden' principle in the *potager*. This allows for the basic layout to be augmented by self-sown herbs and flowers. In one such garden, nasturtiums, cardoons, chicory, chives, rows of leeks alternated with montia, and arches of runner-beans make a stunning show of greenery and flowers.

Another style for a formal vegetable garden which is both ornamental and highly productive is the deep-bed system. The principle is to make a series of beds about 1.5 metres (5 feet) wide (or as far as your arm can comfortably stretch to plant and pick). Each bed is kept richly fertile and densely planted so that the effect is of a mass of waving vegetation. If the beds are double-dug thoroughly when they are first made, they will need little or no digging thereafter, compost or manure being added whenever replanting is carried out. This is an ideal method for those who prefer organic fruit and vegetables but hate to stamp about in the mud; and the planting patterns of vegetable, flowers and fruit can look extremely decorative.

The more traditional kitchen garden with its allotment-style rows can also look pretty, if maintained with meticulous order and preferably some decorative herb or flower borders. On a large or small scale, fruit and vegetables are among the most attractive plants available to a gardener and it is heartening to find imaginative recognition of this fact.

This garden is divided into a number of geometrical box-edged beds, within which flowers and vegetables grow. The principal colour is provided by red poppies and marigolds (used in salads). The oak-leaf lettuce beside the onions is edible and decorative, the lupin, salvia and hollyhock purely ornamental.

ABOVE Flags and bricks or different kinds of brick can be combined to make most attractive patterns. One of the best examples, the Barnsley House *potager* (or kitchen garden) in Gloucestershire, England, is the result of many months of brick-collecting.

This *potager* is one of the best known and most copied in England, an individual interpretation of Villandry on a smaller scale. The shaped beds are edged in dwarf box and dotted with the rose 'Little White Pet' (underplanted with lavender and other flowers and vegetables).

Among the tremendous variety in this garden, generally disparaged foliage, such as spinach, chard and strawberries, makes an ornamental contribution to the overall effect.

A box cone makes a centrepiece with lettuce and ornamental cabbage, and blue daisy-like flowers of chicory are growing on to provide seed for the next year. The cabbages used here are plain-leaved and fringed forms and in pink and white.

OPPOSITE TOP The *potager* at Villandry, ten miles west of Tours, France, extends to 7 hectares (17.3 acres) divided up into nine equal enclosed squares, each of which is made into a different geometrical pattern of box-edged beds, with gravel paths between and rose arbours

at the inner corners. A reconstruction of the original sixteenth-century garden, Villandry continues to be probably the single most important influence on the modern development of the ornamental *potager*.

This vegetable garden was made to be admired: each of the small plots has a colour theme, enhanced with flowers such as petunias, verbena and pansies, each part of a mosaic which has its full effect viewed from the main rooms of the elegant chateau or from the raised walks.

Beds of lush dark onions, coloured blue-green 'Milan' cabbages, small pumpkins and squashes (including the attractive 'Turk's cap' kind), 'Rhubarb' (formerly 'Ruby') chard with its crimson stems, broad beans, aubergines (eggplants), oak-leaved 'Salad Bowl' lettuces and strawberries – all make their contribution to the need for an attractive crop rotation.

ABOVE Dove-grey paths contrast with the large dark leaves of rhubarb in beds around a diamond-shaped centrepiece in this Dutch *potager*. The paths are given raised edges with half bricks, to add an attractive finish and keep the soil from spilling over the paths. Around the sundial are strawberries and lettuce, some of them the red oak-leaved 'Salad Bowl' variety, which is slow to bolt and can be harvested leaf by leaf.

ABOVE LEFT An interesting Dutch *potager*. The striking purple-leaved plants, red orache (*Atriplex hortensis rubra*), have edible leaves, akin to spinach; the snaking green stems in the central plot are Egyptian onions which bear little 'cloves' of onions at the end of each stem. 'Companion' interplanting of French marigolds with carrots is believed to prevent carrot fly depredations.

BELOW LEFT A traditional small English kitchen garden plot with vegetables and a fruit cage, enlivened by the presence of poppies and flowers in the adjacent beds. The very narrow paths are quite sufficient to work from and, with care, you can even get a wheelbarrow through.

ABOVE In the lower part of this garden in Haarlem, Holland, vegetables and flowers mix in easy informality. The flowers of a large borage, reflected in the water bath, are complemented by the tall spikes of delphiniums and what looks like a verbascum, near the gate, nicely setting off the groups of vegetables.

LEFT Prettily patterned paths lead to a trellis with espalier fruit, past a row of the showily dissected foliage of globe artichoke. Beds edged with dwarf box (*Buxus sempervirens* 'Suffruticosa') are further ornamented with large balls of golden box. Quickly cropping lettuce is interplanted between slow-to-mature cabbages.

The precision of the canework for peas makes a virtue out of necessity while the old-fashioned bell jars protecting tender plants are elegant as well as useful. The tiny sprigs of box lining some of the beds are new plants growing on from cuttings taken at pruning time from the larger plants.

ABOVE A purpose-designed wigwam makes a tall focus for this Dutch vegetable garden which uses the flowers and foliage of its vegetables and herbs to create its impact. Here too lettuce (red oak-leaved) is used as a quick crop while the beans begin to make their ascent. The courgette or zucchini behind is starting its succession of large orange flowers, and the silvery-leaved broad-bean clump on the other side of the path will soon be opening its black-blotched white flowers. An outdoor variety of vine, with its decorative leaves, grows up a wooden support, opposite a handsome chicory.

THE
ROSE GARDEN

Rose-growers have a phenomenal treasure at their disposal. The genus *Rosa* includes about a hundred wild species, and cultivars which go back so far that their classification is impossible to ascertain exactly. The garden rose in Europe and America is young beside the forms of Asia, where roses were cultivated at least five thousand years ago.

Rose cultivation is often associated with the British way of life and roses sound a deep resonance in the British consciousness; a complexion of pale beauty is called English Rose, the civil strife of the fifteenth century was known as the Wars of the Roses and finally reconciled under the emblem of the Tudor Rose, a combination of the white York *Rosa × alba* and the red Lancaster *Rosa gallica* var. *officinalis*. The Tudor rose itself was partly inspired by the red and white parti-coloured roses of the time. A gardener of the present day may still choose to grow these historic roses from a total selection which numbers about 2,400 named kinds.

Gardens devoted to roses have become places of pilgrimage all over the world. Visitors flock to Mottisfont Abbey in Hampshire for its old rose display and to the Gardens of the Rose near St Albans in Hertfordshire, both in southern England, La Roseraie du Parc de Bagatelle, and Roseraie de l'Hay les Roses, both near Paris, the Municipal Rose Garden in Rome, the Sangerhausen Rosarium in the German Democratic Republic, and the Parc de la Grange in Geneva. There are famous rose gardens in the USA, Canada and Japan, where native species were used to hybridize with those of Europe and Asia, and good collections also in the southern hemisphere (in Australia and New Zealand, for example), where the rose was taken out by settlers. These great gardens act as models for different styles of rose-growing and a great reservoir of genetic stock for future rose breeding.

Most of us are scarcely aware of the heritage of which we are beneficiaries, but nonetheless almost everyone with a garden has a rose somewhere in it. It seems a shame, however, to restrict oneself to 'Peace' or 'Iceberg' without realizing that there are so many different kinds to choose from, to suit gardens of any size, climate or aspect. There are full-petaled old roses, Bourbons and damasks such as 'Souvenir de la Malmaison' and 'Madame Hardy' which make glorious blousy bushes, an exciting range of single roses of every hue, dainty roses for tubs, and climbers and great ramblers such as 'Paul's Himalayan Musk' or *Rosa filipes* 'Kiftsgate', which will race cumbrously over trees and buildings, covering them with flowers.

The plentiful, muddled flowers of the rambling rose
'Albertine' open a strong pink, paling to blush. This popular
and vigorous rose was introduced in France in 1921 and
grows here in a garden just south of Paris, combining well
with wisteria and Virginia creeper. Its blooms are offset
by the pure white of the pelargonium (geranium) below.

FAR LEFT The side-door of an island cottage in Denmark with a living porch of roses and yellow columbines. To judge by its glowing scarlet, clustered double flowers and dark foliage, the red rose could be 'Paul's Scarlet Climber', a good form to have by a doorway since it blooms well even in slight shade but is not very thorny. Also tolerant of semi-shade is the fragrant 'Madame Alfred Carrière', which carries its deliciously scruffy creamy and palest-pink blooms singly on the stem.

TOP LEFT A generously flowering, greenish *Hydrangea arborescens* and a charming group of pink *Diascia rigescens* are overhung by cascades of white roses of the unusual but very pretty rose 'Adélaide d'Orléans' introduced in 1826.

CENTRE LEFT Luxuriantly flowering roses: 'Paul's Himalayan Musk' merging with *Rosa moschata floribunda* making its way through an old apple tree. The single pink rose in the foreground with white centres and golden stamens is *Rosa* 'Complicata', a rose tolerant of poor soil and shade. In this exceptional rose garden, the roses are never pruned, fed or sprayed with any chemical.

Care is restricted to taking out dead wood and supporting branches which grow too heavy for their original props. This garden is on a soil with high lime content, conventionally considered uncongenial to rose-growing, but it seems nobody ever told the 9–12 m (30–40 ft) ramblers or huge variety of rare shrub roses.

BELOW LEFT 'Adélaide d'Orléans' grows over an arch at the Mottisfont rose garden meeting the deep pink blooms of 'Paul Ricault'. 'Constance Spry' grows up the far wall.

ABOVE A tripod or a simple stout post makes a good support for a climbing rose or shrub rose to display its blooms. The resulting pillar of bloom gives an arresting point of attention in a bed or border, lending height and contrast for other groups of plants. The rose here looks like the climber 'Compassion'; its companions are the statuesque globe thistle *Echinops ritro* – its neat green flowerheads as yet completely bare of the purple petals which will cover it later in the summer – *Anaphalis*, delicate spikes of catnip and perfectly colour-matched geraniums.

RIGHT The beauty of single roses is under-rated, but they can be more subtle and interesting than many of the fulsome, sometimes formless hybrids and floribundas. The flowers of this *Rosa* 'Complicata' vary in colour from the deep pink opening flowers and delicate buds, through to pale blush pink, with a golden brush of stamens left behind after the petals have fallen. A rose of great distinction, it grows here with the deep purple *Anchusa azurea* 'Dropmore', white campanulas and the pretty, soft-leaved yellow foxglove *Digitalis grandiflora*.

LEFT Monet's garden at Giverny, close to the Seine, had many flowers in it – besides the famous water lilies and irises. The scene is part of an area devoted principally to growing roses. Although the exact plants and planting patterns of Monet's original garden have been recorded by his great-grandson by marriage, the species and varieties eventually chosen for the garden (open to the public) are not authentically of the Monet period.

The standard rose, trained attractively on a hooped frame, is the brightly cascading 'Dorothy Perkins', and the bedding roses beneath are a mixture of varieties, some of which are quite modern introductions.

ABOVE This private walled garden in Oxfordshire shows the modern climbing rose 'Compassion', with its pink, yellow-tinged petals, trained up the side of the house. The soft, lime-green foliage is the popular golden acacia (*Robinia pseudoacacia* 'Frisia'), which grows fast and whose glowing colour lightens many a garden. The pink rose in the immediate foreground is the German-bred floribunda called 'Dreamland', introduced just over thirty years ago. It is valued for its compact bushiness and the double blooms which show to excellent effect against its rather dark foliage.

ABOVE A glorious fountain of roses in a surprising garden secreted within the urban sprawl of the north-western French town of Orléans. It belongs to André Eve, a nurseryman who enjoys practising his skills in his own piece of land, where he specializes in roses.

The white rose 'Wedding Day' inherits its beautiful glossy foliage from one of its parents, *Rosa*

sinowilsonii. Of vigorous growth, it is often trained through trees, producing abundant, large single flowers with yellow stamens. Its naturally spreading manner of growth makes it a good subject for training as a standard, held firm by a stout post, or grown up a braced tripod to cascade into a weeping display which conceals the support.

OPPOSITE TOP A pink climbing rose and red bedding roses bloom from a rich mid-green curtain of Virginia creeper and wisteria, showing how a different, more discreet effect can be achieved with a climbing rose. The rose foliage itself is scarcely visible, merging as it does with the other leaves, but the numerous blooms show up clearly.

ABOVE LEFT A full-flowered pale pink rose which looks like the popular modern shrub rose 'Constance Spry' at its full-bloomed best, alongside a neighbouring golden-leaved conifer. The beauty of roses, and especially the detail of individual blooms, can be most fully appreciated against the plain contrasting backdrop of a tree, wall or hedge of box, hornbeam or yew.

ABOVE CENTRE 'Dublin Bay', a deep scarlet rose which looks at its best simply displayed against its own glossy, dark green foliage. A modern climber with an upright habit of growth, it does well against a wall or trained on a post or pillar. It flowers continuously through the summer months, the buds rather darker than the open flowers.

ABOVE RIGHT Deservedly loved for well over a century, this vigorous white climbing rose, 'Félicité et Perpétue', with its clusters of full-petaled creamy flowers, is a joy against a wall. It is rather sparsely thorny, making it a good choice for places such as archways or doorways. The dwarf form of this rose, 'Little White Pet', is also a beauty.

THE
GARDEN ROOM

It is pleasant to be able to spend as much time as possible among plants, enjoying the first brightness of spring or late summer evenings. However, even in the best of climates, inclement weather reduces the time people can enjoyably spend in their gardens. One of the most attractive ways to compensate is to add a sun space, green room or conservatory building onto the house and fill it with plants. Being able to give winter protection and warmth vastly increases the range of species you can grow, while also enabling you to enjoy a flowery winter garden when the weather is bleak.

Garden rooms can be found to suit every type and period of dwelling, though it is often best to shop around for a tailor-made one designed for your particular house, which can turn out to be only a little more expensive than those of modular construction. A little forward planning is required to create that rather special hybrid: a garden room which is comfortable both for plants and people. Basic prerequisites are double-glazing to keep warmth in during cold weather, and several roof vents to let out excessive heat in summer and create the ventilation necessary for healthy plants. Tiled or flagged flooring makes cleaning and watering easier and less messy, and damp-resistant furniture, such as Lloyd loom or bamboo, is both comfortable and practical.

Romantic bougainvilleas, the sophisticated elegance of *Lapageria* in palest pink or white, bewitching (and poisonous) daturas, fragrant wax-like hoyas and the attractive European fan palm, *Chamaerops humilis*, will all do well in a temperate garden room (not dropping below about 7°C or 45°F at night). A built-in flowerbed with soil-heating cables lessens your heating bills in winter, while more room for the roots means watering is rather less of a chore in the summer when, even with blinds, a glasshouse gets very hot. On the other hand, plants in pots may be moved around (and isolated if necessary). The ideal solution is probably a combination: a narrow bed for wall climbers and large pots for other plants . . . and a comfortable sofa with some attractive chairs for you and your guests.

The parrot looks happier than most, perching among the papyrus stems, in this beautiful conservatory (sun space) with its orchids, fruiting grape vine, abutilon and bougainvillea – and the oranges ripening in the corner, considered a treat for parrots. Plants with larger leaves are positioned to cool those which are happier in shade.

BELOW A quiet green corner with an attractive grouping of foliage plants. All of them are very easy to grow, and rapidly climb or trail on any surface.

Mermaid fern (*Rhoicissus*) with its glossy, cut leaves merges with the thick large leaves of *Philodendron erubescens*, making a backdrop for the flowering fuchsia.

The feathery foliage of the asparagus fern *Asparagus densiflorus* 'Sprengeri' also climbs high. Beside it, the variegated fountain of the spider plant, *Chlorophytum capense*, spills over its pot. The tiny plantlets formed on the end of long stems can be pegged down into a pot of compost and rooted.

RIGHT A garden room for plants and people; it serves as a shelter during the winter for tender plants and it is also a place to take one's meals, looking out to the splendid garden.

A vine grows up into the roof area, twining its tendrils along the lateral bars and support wires. Beautifully outlined against the pine cupboard, a shrubby oleander shows its foliage to advantage. This Mediterranean species with its scented flowers should be treated with care as all parts are poisonous. Next to it a large scented-leaf pelargonium (geranium) is already in flower, and pretty crimson and gold abutilon flowers by the window.

FAR LEFT Cane furniture which does not mind the occasional damping when the plants are watered is a good idea for a garden room, where the plants may need watering several times a day during the summer. A floor of slate as here or of tiles is also a good idea for the same reason.

Poinsettia and scented-leaf pelargonium foliage cover the left wall, while an elegant *Ficus benjamina* speckles the corner with dark foliage and a kentia palm, *Howeia fosterana*, looks glossily elegant.

ABOVE LEFT 'Black Hamburg' grapes in heavy bunches and scarlet pelargoniums combine to make a splendidly contrasting display in this delightful plant house. Vines are usually rooted out of doors and led into the glasshouse, where they are trained up the walls and under the roof on neatly pinned wires. An advantage of a vine grown this way is that it creates welcome shade for the other plants, though it takes careful pruning to keep one so trim and attractively fruitful. This variety was planted at Hampton Court towards the end of the reign of William and Mary, where it is still flourishes.

BELOW LEFT An English conservatory (or sun space) with terracotta-coloured floor tiles which go well with the pots and brick and the flowers of the oleander. A cool green atmosphere is created in the intermixture of different textures of fern, fuchsia, orchids and hosta leaves, and a sage stone bust, glimpsed through the foliage, adds a touch of gravity.

ABOVE Flowers within the glasshouse and outside in a garden near Dublin, each as colourful as the other. Through the glass we can see narcissi in flower outdoors, which explains why the plants are so crowded together inside, for this is a time of year when sudden frosts can take off small newly raised plants. They must be kept indoors, and then acclimatized slowly to garden conditions.

Some of the plants, the apricot-coloured *Cymbidium* orchids for example, and *Cyclamen persicum*, are strictly indoor plants in this climate.

However, variegated ground ivy, fuchsia and trailing ivy-leaved pelargonium, having been brought almost to flowering under the shelter of glass, can be planted out into beds and hanging baskets when the weather allows.

RIGHT This conservatory at Wallington in Northumberland is in the charge of The National Trust. Here in the harsh climate of a county on the borders of England and Scotland, with cold winters and short summers, the protection given by a glasshouse is especially welcome. Wallington is famous for its light-coloured, fragrant heliotrope, which is trained up a central support, and for its fuchsias, some of which are very old. The trunk of one of them, the 'Rose of Castile Improved', was found to be more than 23 cm (9 in) in diameter.

The fuchsias which can be seen in this photograph – a familiar bell-like hybrid and a long-tubed Mexican type *Fuchsia fulgens* – have a long way to go before they reach anything approaching that eminent stature.

THE
TERRACED GARDEN

Terracing, a practice almost as 'old as the hills', is both picturesque and practical. Used by farmers and horticulturalists alike, it is the standard way of growing things on difficult, hilly terrain and entails levelling the slope into a procession of broad steps supported by low walls, which are then prepared for planting by adding extra soil and some form of fertilizer.

A first consideration with a terraced garden is access: while the planted terraces descend the hillside like a giant's stairway, the human population needs access on a smaller scale and to this end gardeners have made imaginative use of winding paths and steps of unusual and decorative design. At La Mortola, the famous Hanbury garden on the Italian Riviera, the steep garden plunging into the sea is laced with paths which skein in loops through the flowers and trees. At the same time there is a grand central path which descends axially, with balustraded stairways, ornamentation and urns, and pools and ponds with streamlets trickling between them.

A different approach is taken at Upton House in Warwickshire, England, where the south front consists of a vast paved terrace leading downwards to a spacious lawn. This falls away abruptly to disclose the hitherto concealed terraced gardens: a large vegetable garden; a long, double herbaceous border; a rose garden; and, reached by an impressive, balustraded stairway, several terraces with rock plants growing in the walls. In these dry terraces grow iris, fuschia, broom, berberis and the national collection of certain aster cultivars.

A formalized version of terracing, known as the 'parterre', is currently undergoing a fashionable revival. The parterre is a large terrace, divided into symmetrical patterns of beds, usually box-edged, with flowers, herbs or coloured gravels within them. They are now practicable in a modern garden, owing to the new ways of managing weeding and clipping which reduce maintenance to a minimum.

Even within a flat landscape, where a garden is restricted to one terrace only, spatial surprises can be contrived. A single terrace may be designed to be on the same level as the living rooms of the house, to enable people to pass smoothly from indoors to outdoors. The single terrace is a paved, sociable area, ideally decorated with statuary and pots of eye-catching plants such as lilies, cordylines and small trees.

This breathtakingly beautiful garden in north-west France, once the home of French painter Henri le Sidanier, is on too elaborate a scale for most of us, but we can take note of some of the details – how red and pink roses are set off by grey stone, how walls of differing heights, balustrades, evergreens and trees play their part.

ABOVE Hard-wearing engineering bricks give the path and steps a honey-coloured glow – the brightly planted borders on either side seem insubstantial against such solidity. Annuals, perennials, shrubs and trailing plants make a diverse mixture of colours and shapes. *Campanula latifolia* and lupins find an echo in the lower spires of pink antirrhinum (snapdragon). The rose bush, a more permanent fixture, is underplanted with petunias while bright yellow creeping Jenny brightens the retaining wall. Mimulus shouts its presence and, to the left of the steps, blooms the pretty *Campanula persicifolia*.

RIGHT A small garden only 12 × 12 m (40 × 40 ft) designed on several levels can be exciting and interesting. Earth excavated in one part can be piled to make higher levels elsewhere. Hard-edged steps and walls richly planted with evergreens and flowering plants give a soft lush multi-tiered impression. In this garden the ivies 'Buttercup' and 'Tricolor' – with a cream margin which turns purple in autumn – grow in two tiers. The variegated *Lamium* 'Beacon Silver' with pink stubby flowers and lamb's ears (*Stachys byzantina*) brighten the steps. Boundary trellising, supporting climbers, adds height and privacy.

LEFT Foliage makes the predominant effect chosen for this sheltered terrace. Statuesque oleander and agave in pots, with clipped box and bay, and euphorbia and *Helleborus foetida* on either side of the steps, contrast with plants of a looser texture such as wisteria and dainty meadow rue in the foreground. Variegated ivy, *Senecio* and other grey-leaved plants set off the contrast.

ABOVE FAR LEFT A neat and pretty garden with shallow steps and a stepped rock garden. An interesting contrast is created by featuring a single apple with a gold-leaved tree, probably cut-leaved elder. Gold and orange annuals – fiery French and African marigolds – contrast with soft-coloured lavender, candytuft and alchemilla. The bright effect of the whole is increased by contrast with the darker greens of the woodland.

BELOW FAR LEFT A roofed canopy neatly divides this most colourful garden as well as giving covered access between the barn and the house. The wide, slowly ascending path makes a delightful pale contrast for the strong plant colours: red valerian looking all the brighter against the greens of male fern and tall euphorbia (*Euphorbia characias* subsp. *wulfenii*). Above, growing on the black barn, a glorious 'Gloire de Dijon' blooms luxuriantly, in companionship with hybrid clematis. Under the arch, on the dry edge to the path, just before the next steps, the sisyrhinchium (*S. striatum*) gleams palely against a mass of softly merging colours, backed by the pink pipes of tall foxgloves.

BELOW A dramatic linear garden in temperate New Zealand, which merges into the countryside with its distant mountains. Terraces are ranged on either side of a long axial brick path. The eye, drawn down by an urn on the lowest level, is diverted by the terracotta pots with their cargo of pelargoniums (geraniums). Tall columnar trees, such as fastigiate yew, work well in a linear scheme, holding the design together and accentuating levels like giant exclamation marks. Much use is made of the textures of grey and silvery foliage, which match the grey stone and set off the bright golds, reds and oranges.

RIGHT A delicious late afternoon after a baking late summer day, the high gravelled terrace surrounded by cushions of Virginia creeper *Parthenocissus tricuspidata*, which is the species most favoured in France. This is the one which colours so richly in the autumn, when the mounded creeper on the walls and the gabled side of the tiled building beyond makes a perpetual sunset around the terrace until the frosts and winds of winter take away the leaves. In summer, additional colour is provided by red valerian (at the foot of the steps) and a patch of bright annuals which encircle the tree.

RIGHT A gradually ascending garden full of colour in mixed beds. *Lavatera* 'Silver Cup', a bright pink, very flowery annual, grows to a tall bush from seed sown in early spring. *Rudbeckia* (also treated as an annual) gives one of the brightest of summer gold-yellows, and other bedding plants, such as antirrhinums (snapdragons), dianthus, *Kochia* and phlox, extend the range of colour. More permanent plants include roses and butterfly bushes, while Virginia creeper and wisteria are covering the wall of the house. The garden, with its many annual plants, reaches a colourful climax in high summer.

FAR RIGHT A formal garden created from a field in fifteen years. The armillary sphere (used by early astronomers to determine star position and by modern gardeners as an elaborate sundial) was contrived by Cecil Beaton. The eye is led to an upper level through a pair of gate pier capitals on square bases, their verticals echoed by the slender fastigiate yews, along a beech *allée* rising to the obelisk. Throughout, the impact of the garden ornament is reinforced by the plants: trees and hedges, the curves of the grass and even the soft, grey leaves of the sages edging the grey stone flags.

THE
SCENTED GARDEN

Scent is arguably the most evocative of all sensual stimuli and an essential in any garden. So all gardens should be scented ones, reaching towards an ideal orchestration of the most poignantly perfumed plants, subtly combining and recombining with different tones and new voices over the whole season. A large part of the skill in creating a scented garden comes in choosing places not only where the different plants will thrive, but also where people can enjoy them to most advantage.

The flowers of winter – the scented viburnums such as the tiny pink clusters of *Viburnum* × *bodnantense*, the fragrant *Daphne laureola*, or the tiny bright gold ribbons of witch hazel – are keenly appreciated on the chill air, but you need to be quite close so the warmth of your breath increases the scent. Winter honeysuckle, *Lonicera fragrantissima*, has a stronger fragrance and planted around a doorway will thrill many a visitor. In milder areas if you plant a winter-flowering honeysuckle and white jasmine on either side of the door, you can enjoy scent for much of the year.

As the weather begins to warm with the spring, the small clustery pink flowers of *Daphne mezereum* open. Their scent is heavy enough but often lost on the wind unless you pick the flowers or bury your face in them. The tossing, heavy heads of lilac fill the air of early summer. *Clematis montana* with its vanilla-scented flowers (which last much longer in shady places) brings in high summer, accompanied by the richness of pearly white summer jasmine and *Lilium regale*. As autumn draws on and the temperature cools, there is the erotic spiciness of acidantheras, the small sweet blooms of the holly-like shrub *Osmanthus heterophyllus* or the fast-growing *Elaeagnus* × *ebbingei*.

Roses are always associated with high summer, but with so many kinds to choose from you can ensure fragrant blooms from spring up to the frosts – but make sure to choose scented varieties as some have little or no fragrance. Old roses such as 'Souvenir de la Malmaison' and 'Madame Hardy' are exceptionally generous, and the briars and *Rosa primula* have the advantage of deliciously scented leaves.

Some plants, herbs and scented pelargoniums (geraniums), divulge their scents only when the foliage or flowers are pressed or trodden on. Scented bushes such as lavenders, or rosemary, can be planted along pathways, where you brush them as you walk by. Large pots of scented pelargoniums with the perfumes of lemon, balsam, pine resin and spiced oranges and a sprinkling of tiny pink and white flowers make excellent entrance and doorstep sentinels.

Much has been written about chamomile lawns but they are fearfully difficult and fiddly to maintain, and it is perhaps better to incorporate this charming plant (the non-flowering variety, 'Treneague') into a herb seat, or plant a small patch in a place where people stand at a gate or by a doorway. A pretty shrub called *Cercidiphyllum* has round leaves which turn crimson-brown in the autumn and have a delicious scent which recalls afternoons spent cooking sugar to make brittle toffee, but only when tucked into a glove or warmed in a pocket.

This trellised arbour, sheltering a classical statue from
Vicenza which represents summer, is laced with summer
flowering plants: climbing roses, clematis and honeysuckle.
The centrepiece for a secluded scented garden of roses,
honey-sweet lilies and lavender, it is reached through a
tracery of small winding paths.

ABOVE A scented garden corridor thickly lined with densely planted lavender, which makes a splendid contrast with the glossy dark leaves of paeony and the dark green bushiness of the espaliered apples trained up the righthand wall. A few spires of tall delphinium rise up by the opposite wall, continuing the lavender-mauve theme.

The lavender is probably the variety known as 'Hidcote', which is often used ornamentally because it is compact and has good dark purple-blue flower spikes. To create this formal, even effect, it is best to select small lavenders about the same height, and plant them out at the same time, about 23 cm (9 in) or so apart. They like a well-drained soil which is not too rich, in a sunny position.

Once the hedge is established, the dead flowerheads should be removed when they begin to fade in late summer, and light trimming carried out. Older plants which begin to straggle should be cut back hard to promote growth in early spring.

Lavenders tend to get uneven and leggy as they age, and need replanting every five or six years. They can be propagated from cuttings taken from non-flowering shoots, rooted in a peat and sand mixture, and grown on in a cold frame for the winter, then planted *in situ* the following autumn or early spring.

Flowering spikes required for drying or making into lavender bags should be picked before they are fully out. Long stems with the flowers just showing colour are best. They can be dried simply in small sheaves, tied with string and hung up in a warm, dry (but not sunny) place.

TOP RIGHT Two large clumps of lavender make a scented frame at the top of some rustic, brick steps. It is a good idea to place scented plants near a path or doorway, where people can brush them as they pass.

Lavender is also one of the very best plants for scent when it is dried. Only a few are needed to make a strong contribution to a potpourri. For a lavender bag, the dried flowers are removed and sewn into a cotton bag. Alternatively, the stems of a small bundle can be tied beneath the flowers, and the long soft, stems

carefully bent back and secured. Threading a ribbon in and out of the stems finishes the 'lavender bottle', which freshens drawers of clothes for a long time.

ABOVE RIGHT *Nicotiana alata* growing by a doorway. The flowers open at night, releasing their fragrance on the evening air. The whitish flowered sorts are better than the new varieties, which are more brightly coloured but unscented. The plants themselves are rather floppy but worth growing for the scent.

The dead flowerheads should be taken off as they fade, a slightly unpleasant job since they are rather sticky to handle, but it improves the general appearance of the plants and encourages new flowers, thus extending the blooming period.

Nicotianas are usually treated as fairly tender annuals, sown inside at the end of winter – they need a temperature of about 18°C (64°F). After being carefully acclimatized to cooler conditions, they should be planted outside only after any danger of frost has passed.

TOP The rose 'New Dawn', which was introduced from America in the 1930s, was very widely planted in England after World War II, at least partly because its name represented a potent symbol.

However, it has many other qualities to recommend it. 'New Dawn' is a very attractive climber, with its glossy dark foliage, habit of flowering more or less continuously all summer, and tolerance of poor soils and moderate shading. The dark pink buds open to paler pink blooms with a gentle fragrance.

ABOVE LEFT A soft-coloured and sweet-scented association of honeysuckle and the rambling rose 'Albertine'. The honeysuckle is probably *Lonicera japonica,* which is vigorous and bears fragrant flowers from summer until autumn.

ABOVE RIGHT Such an effect can be achieved by using a dark honeysuckle such as *Lonicera periclymenum* with a dark pink double rose such as 'Cardinal Hume', a strongly scented small shrub or 'Veilchenblau', a climber with purple-pink flowers.

RIGHT A beautiful deep border in summer: scented roses and honeysuckle, with campanulas, and poppies just about to flower. The white froth in the centre is *Clematis recta*, which grows to about 1–2 m (3–6 ft). The garden's owner feels it is rather too floppy to be desirable as a garden plant, except perhaps in the purple form which has very good spring shoots. A very good clematis with creamy-white blossoms is *Clematis flammula*, a vigorous climber with a strong, heady scent. It comes into flower in late summer.

This garden surrounds (and almost obscures) a thatched cottage in the Isle of Wight. The time is early summer as the first roses come out and the lilacs reach perfection.

The common lilac is native to eastern Europe but it grows well in Britain and other temperate climates, reaching a height of 3 m (10 ft) or more and an even wider spread. In Holland there is a considerable trade in lilac bloom brought on under glass, but in Britain a traditional and very widespread superstition that it is unlucky to bring lilac flowers into the house has affected its popularity as a cut flower.

It is, however, much grown in gardens, with many handsome named varieties available ('Madame Lemoine', a double, and 'Vestale' are good white examples). The flowers should be removed as they fade, and thin or crossing branches cut out in autumn, when overlarge shoots can also be shortened to encourage new shoots (though these will take a few years to flower). Suckers which spring up from the base of the trunk should be removed as soon as they appear.

This is the south-eastern corner of a walled garden, open to the public, at Capel Manor in Middlesex, twelve miles to the north of London. The wide paths make it hospitably accessible so that people can easily walk two or three abreast and there is also plenty of room for wheelchair visitors to manoeuvre safely.

In summer it is the sight and scent of old-fashioned roses such as Bourbons, damasks and musks, all highly fragrant, and grown as bush, pillar and bedding plants, which dominate the display. Inside a walled garden, scent is amplified, so that the heavy, warm fragrance of rose and lavender meets you as soon as you set foot within.

People always try to cut corners so edging beds with lavender ensures that there is a continuous fragrance on the air. Bearded irises are generally extolled for the complex beauty of their flowers rather than their scent but earlier in the summer, when there are fewer strong-smelling competitors, keen-nosed gardeners know and value their characteristic and curiously piquant fragrance.

THE
SHADED GARDEN

The subtle pleasures of the shady garden – dappled shadows, inviting depths, the quiet interplay of foliage and flower – are becoming increasingly appreciated as gardeners draw on more imaginative ideas and the greater accessibility of exciting plants. One of the prime advantages of the shaded garden is that the light does not alternately dazzle and fade: it is clear and consistent, bringing out the individual qualities of the plants.

Thoughtful choice and positioning of plants which tolerate and thrive in shaded conditions can change a chilly, dark space into a cool, green refuge starred with flowers in spring and summer, while in the coldest weather, evergreens and scented winter-flowering species create a sheltered, verdant atmosphere. There is a wide range of flowering plants, shrubs and trees which originated in woodland and other overshadowed natural habitats and will only do well in shaded conditions. Others we regard as sun-lovers readily adopt and reward the shade gardener with a longer flowering period and more perfect blooms.

Plants with cream, shell pink, pale lilac, and, in particular, white flowers create their own luminosity and are especially effective at twilight, which is often the only time when many working people can enjoy their gardens during the week. More flamboyant effects can be achieved by using brightly coloured plants: winter aconites, crocuses, primroses and grape hyacinths for the spring, closely followed by the dazzling gold of leopard-bane. Different coloured kinds of corydalis and dicentras contribute soft mounds of fern-like foliage as well as distinctive flowers.

Lilies are not usually considered shady plants but many wood-dwellers such as Turk's caps and the Pyrenean lily will do well, as also do the delectable dog-tooth violets with their clear colours and thrown-back flowerheads. Some fritillaries, such as the greeny-purple *Fritillaria pontica* or even the snake's-head fritillary, will hold their strangely beautiful blooms for a long time in sheltered shade. Later in the year there are the strange speckled *Tricyrtis* (toad lilies) and graceful Japanese anemones to look forward to.

Evergreen plants can keep the garden attractive in the winter months, for example: yew and box, which can be shaped or made into hedges; juniper with its scented foliage, in all kinds of cultivated shapes and forms; flowering shrubs such as choisya and osmanthus, which have sweet-smelling flowers as well as good foliage; and ivies in glossy, rippled, gold or silver-splashed foliage to drape walls, fences or steps.

A lovely community of shady plants: the formal box and
yew contrasting with the free arches of Solomon's seal,
cabbagey bergenia foliage, the wide pleats of hosta and the
star-like hellebore leaves. Variegated *Euonymus fortunei*
brightens the pathside and *Hydrangea petiolaris* drapes the
wall under the pretty rowan foliage.

ABOVE LEFT This Dutch garden shows what can be achieved in a shady plot of land by contrasting shapes and textures of foliage of different tones. Natural contrasts are augmented by using trained and clipped forms.

The unusual clipped conifer balls trimmed as standards with bare trunks, clipped yew and carafe-shaped box and the two lightly clipped grey santolinas give the garden its 'bone structure'. The 'free-form' plants include hosta, bergenia and ferns, speckled with flowers of viola, allium, poppies and a few roses.

BELOW A shaded garden which has to complement this rather elegant building in Amsterdam. The planting has been done in the shade thrown by a cedar tree, one of the most difficult trees to plant beneath.

The gently rising brick path leads through a shade-tolerant mixture of perennials, small trees and shrubs, with light and open foliage.

Flower colours are restricted to a range of pale pinks, fawns and greenish-creams which merge with the pale foliage – except for the rhododendron with its dark foliage and cerise flowers.

BELOW FAR LEFT Glossy green bouquets of bird's-nest fern with its wide leaves and the narrower leaved, crinkled hart's-tongue (an easy fern to grow) are rarely given prominence, but look most attractive in this cool, overcast area of a small town garden. The elegant fronds behind look as if they belong to the ostrich fern *Matteuccia struthiopteris*, a most beautiful fern for the garden and one which can grow to well over 1m (3ft) in height by autumn.

There are several delightful aconites with white flowers. This one has creamy-coloured spikes of bloom floating above the leaves; it would seem to be a small cultivar called 'Ivorine', which is a lovely plant for cool and shaded conditions.

BELOW LEFT A most appealing grouping of plants, most of them readily available and easily grown. They make a lush green sea of foliage and flower around a simple, rough bench in this small town garden. Spires of yellow loosestrife, *Lysimachia punctata*, bloom in late summer, and in shade hold their flowers for a longer time than those which are grown in a sunny position.

Two hostas with creamy margins (possibly 'Thomas Hogg') stand out against the surrounding foliage. In front of each, the grass gardener's garters *Phalaris arundinacea* 'Picta' (attractive but very rampant) makes spiky variegated ribbons with spear-like leaves of iris to the right and the rounded bergenia to the left.

ABOVE RIGHT The brighter the sun, the deeper the shade, as shown in this Australian garden, around the front of an old colonial building. The tree with its starry, glossy palmate leaves is the sweetgum *Liquidambar styraciflua* (not in fact an Australian native but from the Americas). Like a green fountain on a mossy pillar, the tree fern *Cyathea australis* (which is more commonly known by its old name *Dicksonia*) makes a wonderful plumey show, as does the variegated grass *Chlorophytum comosum* 'Milky Way' caught in a fleck of bright sun.

BELOW RIGHT An impressive combination of flower and foliage: the saw-leaved *Helleborus argutifolius* (which was *H. corsicus*) with its heavy green cups beside the frothy white candles of *Tiarella cordifolia*, with ferns adding extra texture.

FAR RIGHT A tree canopy of copper and silver leaves above an unusually flowery shade-garden. The brightest flowers, the plumed astilbes, do very well in shaded conditions. The glowing pink shows up better than the stouter dark-red variety in front of them. Other pale pinks dot the garden: toadflax (*Linaria purpurea* 'Canon Went'), hydrangea and *Geranium macrorrhizum*.

The golden spires lurking beside the hydrangea make a quietly dramatic impact; though it is difficult to make them out clearly, they look as if they are *Ligularia stenocephala* 'The Rocket'. Green-gold at ground level is provided by the ubiquitous *Alchemilla mollis*, which will grow and flower quite well in shade.

LEFT A cleverly banked effect of greens, creams and golds. Golden marjoram at the lowest level mingles with golden flowers of *Alchemilla mollis*, behind which the buttery gold of the buttercup-like *Trollius* blends with fawny-yellow foxgloves.

To the left, the white-spotted foliage of pulmonaria leads back to the greyish feathery foliage and white daisy-like flowers (possibly *Argyranthemum*), a creamy lupin and several kinds of foxgloves: common white, small *Digitalis lutea* and *D. grandiflora*.

The next tier includes variegated shrubs, and an unusual centrepiece, next to the *Aruncus dioicus* (the flowers of which resemble an ivory-flowered bottlebrush) – the plume poppy *Macleaya cordata* just about to flower. This plant, which can reach nearly 2 m (5–6 ft), carries its pearl-white blooms in tall plumy panicles.

TOP A surprising artificial grass bank with spiral box topiary seeming to hold back a bed of green foliage.

ABOVE A brooding eagle by a small pool looks down towards the house through a patchwork of low ferns, ivies, lamium and plants of variegated foliage growing at the base of birch trees, which give the garden a consistent gentle shade.

THE
COTTAGE GARDEN

The cottage-garden style means generous planting, a luxuriant blending of colour and foliage. It represents a scene of rural bliss: a sea of blooms through which a path leads to the cottage door, where a young woman stands in the sun, a child at her knee and at her feet ducks with plumage white as the lilies. The pure accents of white roses and campanulas and the startling white bar on a chaffinch's wing complete the scene. This vision is familiar from the paintings of Helen Allingham, whose work was romantic, evocative and so precise that not only species but also varieties of plant can be identified with complete confidence.

Certain plants are always associated with cottage gardens: Madonna lilies, hollyhocks, lupins, Canterbury bells, irises, Virginia stocks, lavender, Michaelmas daisies. Honeysuckle and jasmine grow in and over walls and hedges, or, like roses, are allowed to tumble down over steps or arch over doorways. In the gardens of a century or so ago, though less so in modern reconstructions, there were soft fruit such as currants, gooseberries and raspberries and tree fruit such as apples and pears, while vegetables such as lettuces, onions, broad beans and cabbage were grown in neat rows alongside parsley, rosemary and chives.

The controlled luxuriance of the cottage garden is particularly attractive to people living in times in which the outward signs of civilization are standardization and mass production. It appeals to our technological age as much as it did to the Victorians of the Industrial Revolution. Then, as now, the word 'cottage' covered a wide range of description, from poverty-stricken labourers' dwellings to nicely kept village houses and rural retreats, and was applied also to small farmhouses and suburban villas. The gardens extolled in Helen Allingham's paintings, the writing of Flora Thompson and by the influential landscape gardener William Robinson (who started a magazine called *The Country Garden* in 1892) were idealized visions of rural contentment. Commitment to this style of gardening for over a century has contrived to keep many attractive 'cottage garden' varieties of plants alive, enabling the cottage gardens of today to be as beautiful and nostalgic as those of the past.

Nothing beckons quite so invitingly as an open gate:
beyond, wall shrubs and day lilies, and in the borders blue
campanula, several kinds of rose and an unusual columbine.
The busy *Alchemilla mollis* and geraniums tumble over the
grass. Long, narrow gardens gain intimacy if they are
divided into two compartments by a thick hedge of
honeysuckle or box or a low wall.

ABOVE LEFT The cottage garden with its gently blended flowers, fruit and vegetable plants which became Gold Medal and overall winner of the model gardens at the Chelsea Flower Show in London, 1988. Designed and planted by Jacqui Moon and John Ravenscroft for the Women's Institute, this 'Countrywoman's Garden' was clearly the most attractive of the more naturalistic style show gardens at this prestigious horticultural event.

Roses grew up the weathered picket fence, broad beans rubbed shoulders with vermilion paeonies. A simple brick and cinder path was edged with herbs and flowers such as blue and pink-pastel columbines and Russell lupins. On one side was a white-boarded beehive, on the other, a conical, clipped bay tree. There was rhubarb and two large, old-fashioned, terracotta forcing pots – ornamental and useful. This garden was based on Jacqui Moon's country garden.

ABOVE CENTRE This handsome cottage in ornamental flint and brick hardly requires decoration, but on a grey day flowering climbers make a welcome show. Honeysuckle, which tries to envelope everything once it becomes established, is restrained, bushing out at the corner, a long garland over the window. Below, the dainty white flowers of Mexican orange blossom (*Choisya ternata*) make a mound of pale contrast against its glossy evergreen leaves.

TOP RIGHT A mixture of vegetables, herbs and flowers growing in happy luxuriance, given shape by a low box hedge and a rose arch, which frames the view up the path to the cottage door. A slender standard (long-stemmed) box rises above the lavender in the centrally placed tub.

The owner, having viewed the garden from each room of the house in turn, embarked on a 'two-year plan' which she is still working on twenty years later. There are borders and herbs, vegetables, roses and shrubs, even an attractive standard gooseberry. Close to the gate the tall broad beans with grey-green foliage mask the large leaves of variegated horseradish.

By next season the roses ('Pink Cloud') will have met over the arch at the entrance and the climbing rose by the green-flowered hydrangea will have grown up the side of the house, by which time other plans will no doubt be afoot.

ABOVE RIGHT A corner of a small cottage garden within a large estate in southern England. The milky-white fragrant *Philadelphus* 'Belle Etoile' has four petals arranged almost as a square with a tuft of golden stamens, a small purplish blotch at the very centre. It is an easy-going shrub which thrives in sun or partial shade. These young plants, with tall delphiniums between them, will reach 2.5–3 m (8–10 ft) in a few years, hiding the pink rose 'François Juranville'.

The fierce white of the orange-blossom 'Virginal' is answered boldly by the brilliant scarlet flowerheads of the Maltese Cross *Lychnis chalcedonica*. The strong pinks of roses and bright yellow of loosestrife each make their own point. Blue and white Canterbury bells and delphinium hybrids intensify the picture.

This garden in Oxfordshire in southern England has its own dramatic identity within the cottage-garden style of plant selection and luxuriant growth. Although this delightful profusion of flowers looks naturally haphazard, it soon becomes evident that this garden has been carefully planted, pruned and tended to achieve the apparently casual, even unruly effect, colour matching colour in ascending tiers of bloom.

Biennials such as Canterbury bells are sown in autumn or early spring for planting outdoors the next October, to flower the summer of the year afterwards. Most twentieth-century roses require feeding and pruning to flower freely. For perennial patches to be shapely and not territorialize space reserved for other plants, they need judicious restraint. This is not a high-expenditure garden but that of someone who loves plants and enjoys raising and tending them. Named cultivars of roses should be bought from a reputable dealer, but orange-blossom and other plants grow easily from cuttings, and friends are always willing to donate a cheery spreading plant such as yellow loosestrife.

ABOVE A garden on heavy clay in the south of England, with generously flowering plants, bright against the grey stone. A sea of purple *Campanula poscharskyana* washes around pink oriental poppies and *Diascia* spires. Hostas and *Alchemilla mollis* bush out over the path, while a variegated euonymus (*Euonymus fortunei* 'Silver Queen') grows behind another clump of poppies.

A stone vase blotched with orange lichens adds to the attractiveness of this delightfully informal scene – not part of the most recent revival of cottage plants but a place which has been a true cottage garden for years and years.

LEFT A pastel interpretation of the cottage-garden ideal using flowers and foliage: pinks, lilac-blue, soft white and grey-green melt gently into one another. Soft colours can easily become a dull blur, but here the effect is given definition – spiky grey foliage (*Anaphalis* and artemisia) makes pale highlights among the green leaves.

Although it is rather difficult to name the individual flowers with conviction, they seem to be the lilac-purple variety of the obedient plant, *Physostegia virginiana*, pink umbrellas of a verbena hybrid (though *Achillea* would look similar) and white puffs of *Anaphalis triplinervis*.

ABOVE The owner of this streamside garden in a valley not far from the sea in south-west England has solved the problem of integrating sweet peas into a garden, so that you get the benefit of their beauty and scent without the penalty of an ugly structure of bamboos or trellis.

The rustic tent-pole effect, imaginative, simple and practical, makes an attractive feature out of a potential eyesore, and moreover creates a tall and colourful backcloth of flowers and foliage for the rest of this flowerbed.

The owner's object is principally to find new and interesting colour associations using a combination of

annuals and some perennials. The bold orange heads of the annual French marigolds (*Tagetes patula* cultivars) and the feathery-leaved daisy-like cosmos will have to be either bought or raised from seed and planted out each spring in their place behind the perennial lavender.

The creamy orange, golds and deeper reds of the marigolds make a strong, bright patch of colour, an adventurous stroke which enlivens the muted pink-purple. At the front of the bed pink-headed candytuft (*Iberis umbellata*), another hard-working annual, blends its colour beautifully with the lavender.

LEFT A quiet and shady corner at the end of a secluded garden has been created by its owners, first by establishing tall hedges around the boundary of their property, then by planting roses and other plants for an extended succession of bloom through the summer. The ubiquitous 'Iceberg' floribunda flowers almost continuously through the summer. The lax single blooms of the pink shrub rose make a once only but beautiful summer show amongst grey-leaved coronaria and linaria.

Two modern climbing roses make a gleaming white sprawl over the rooftop – possibly 'Kiftsgate' (a very vigorous form of *Rosa filipes*) and

'Seagull' (a *Rosa multiflora* hybrid) which also has very strong dense growth. Both have the characteristic of growing well in partial shade.

ABOVE This pretty vegetable garden in Kendal in the north of England includes rows of flowers for cutting as well as food plants. The sweet peas are here grown on long twiggy branches stuck down well into the ground, which make a natural-looking support for their clinging tendrils. The leafy neatness of the rows of leeks and beets, and the pale block of lettuce, has its own attraction, while pompom dahlias will provide blooms for the house.

ABOVE A curving path of circular stepping stones gives the impression of a mysterious destination beyond. It is a design which makes any garden seem larger. Chamomile has been planted around and between the stones, so a sweet apple-sweet fragrance is created with every footfall. The kind usually planted for lawns and niches is the flat, non-flowering 'Treneague' but here the owner has put in the double-flowered chamomile, which stays low where it is trodden upon but grows taller and flowers on each side of the pathway.

In this part of the garden the level of plants, shrubs and trees is kept low. When trees outgrow their space, they are moved (the pine to the left has now been replaced with a spiral box). The soil is very poor so plants such as lilies are raised in large containers which are sunk in the ground, but astilbes, such as the pale pink one on the left, the many alliums with their deep pink flowerheads (on the right), and the crimson-leaved Japanese maple seem able to thrive given compost and careful feeding throughout the growing season.

ABOVE A small cottage garden in Kent, in south-eastern England, which is designed and planted to give a sense of seclusion and greater size. Arches, small brick pillars, terracotta pots, simply clipped box and paths set the outlines. The carefully-placed bench, half overgrown with flowers, is a place to look towards as well as somewhere to rest and look outwards.

Within the confines of the beds, the planting is informal, with herbs, lilies and field poppies mixed together. The poppies usually require no planting, once the first few are established, because they self-seed as well in a garden as they did in old crop fields. Since wildflower gardens have become popular, it is easier to obtain the field poppy *Papaver rhoeas*. The

mixed pastels of the Shirley strain (which can also be double-flowered) are pretty but lack the simple drama of the wild red poppy.

Roses which climb through trees are extremely impressive, but it is important to make sure before planting that the rose is not ever going to grow too large and weighty for its living support.

THE COLOUR-THEME GARDEN

Gertrude Jekyll, the most influential exponent of colour-theme gardens, was an embroiderer and painter as well as a practical gardener and garden designer. She found it 'extremely interesting to work out gardens in which some special colouring predominates' and, pleased with her success in making a grey garden, wrote, 'it opens out a whole new range of garden delights . . . besides my small grey garden I badly want others, and especially a gold garden, a blue garden and a green garden'.

One of the most famous single-colour gardens and the one most copied is Vita Sackville-West's elegant white garden at Sissinghurst in Kent, England, successful because the design incorporated not simply the pure, hard whites which tend to glare but also cream and silver-white flowers, and silver foliage such as willow-leaved pear and artemisia, and statuesque thistles. She blended and contrasted flowers and foliage of varying shapes and textures: white lungwort, variegated phlox, the white-flowering burning bush (*Dictamnus albus*), white and creamy-white bush roses, silvery lamb's ears (*Stachys byzantina*, also known as *S. lanata*), and a large rambling *Rosa longicuspis* arching over a pergola.

Unadulterated themes of blue or purple look dull, and pinks insipid, but in combination they give a warmly glowing effect. The catnip *Nepeta* 'Six Hills Giant' makes a long-flowering edging, and the tall, purple *Verbena bonariensis* looks especially well with a range of lavenders, penstemmons, campanulas and roses, with both blue and pink species geraniums to set them off. *Salvia patens* is not hardy except in the mildest climates but it has the clearest, deepest end-of-season blue, combining well with the blue-purple of the hardy ceratostigmas in a lovely, late summer show.

It is more difficult to design with the harder, brasher colours but a successful effect can be achieved by limiting the palette to three or four strong colours and contrasting the boldest effects – for example, red sedums and purple berberis with the golden *Achillea* 'Moonshine'. Aggressive colours such as these need tempering with a few pale silvery-leaved plants such as *Ballota* or artemisia. Another approach to a 'hot border' uses scarlet, yellow and white flowers – against the dark blaze red and purple foliage.

This garden in a limestone region of Somerset, in the west of England, continues to develop, while keeping to the spirit of Gertrude Jekyll's design. Originally featuring tall roses, this section now has rich purple *Clematis* × Jackmanii climbing over tall supports and spilling down to mingle with different varieties of lavender.

LEFT The Sissinghurst white garden in Kent, England, has been the model for many other large and small-scale gardens. Enclosed by a hedging of tall yew, creams, greys and whites glow ethereally. Divided internally by small box hedges and paths of flagstone and brick, each bed is packed full with interesting and unusual plants. The garden exploits grey foliage plants: the tall silvery-grey willow-leaved pear tree, artemisias, lavender and hostas. At the centre is the great umbrella of the rampant white *Rosa longicuspis*.

TOP An elegant garden bench focuses attention on a particular aspect of the scene and provides a practical resting place. This one at the famous garden of Hidcote in Gloucestershire, in the west of England, is surrounded by a canopy of the white rose 'Nevada', with a low-growing complement of *Anthemis cupaniana*, an attractive Italian relative of chamomile.

ABOVE LEFT In the leafy fullness of early summer, creamy white wisteria provides the principal drama in this subdued palette of light green foliage.

The pale, verdant spikiness of the wisteria leaves is perfectly balanced in the colour and leaf-shape of the tree paeony to the left.

ABOVE RIGHT A creamy astilbe makes a fountain of bloom behind this white-flowered tableau of plants. Mop-heads of dazzling phlox lean in from the left over subtly green-tinged nicotiana, while at the lowest level the ivory-flowered *Anaphalis*, with its blue grey leaves, looks slightly muddy against the vivid greens and snowy-white brilliance.

ABOVE Daffodils, narcissi, spring squill (*Scilla sibirica*) and many kinds of flat-cupped narcissi naturalize readily in the grass beneath trees of a copse or old orchard. My own opinion is that true species or early-blooming hybrids look better than large 'artificial' cultivars.

The true wild daffodils, *Narcissus pseudonarcissus*, with their nervous, alert beauty, are now more widely available. They should be planted slightly more deeply in turf and left alone when they establish themselves.

The scented poet's narcissus, *Narcissus poeticus*, is an attractive European narcissus with white petals and a flat dark orange cup. The old variety 'Pheasant's Eye' (*Narcissus poeticus* 'Recurvus'), which has a slight greenishness within the cup, is both beautiful and fragrant. A cultivar which looks particularly well planted in drifts in the grass is the golden 'Peeping Tom' with its thrown-back petals and neat, narrow corona.

The most popular squill is the deep blue variety 'Spring Beauty' or 'Atrocoerulea', which thrives in dappled shade. It should be left undisturbed to increase year by year (a light top dressing of leaf mould in late summer aids flowering).

TOP RIGHT A glowing combination on a south-facing wall in the old kitchen garden at Powis Castle on the Welsh border. The creamy-yellow rose 'Lawrence Johnston', with its semi-double fragrant flowers and light green foliage, is a strong variety which would also grow well in other less sunny aspects. The soft, powdery rich blue of the ceanothus growing beneath the rose will spread to nearly 2 m (6 ft) on a sheltered sunny wall (grown in the open it makes a small bushy shrub). This one, *Ceanothus foliosus*, is regarded as not reliably hardy below −12°C (10°F) so is best grown against the shelter of a wall except in the very mildest regions.

ABOVE RIGHT A summer scene rich with the deepest blues and yellows. Foreground delphiniums tone with the purple of dense small spires of floriferous dwarf salvia called 'East Friesland'. These are best in good, fertile soil in a sunny position.

The bright flowers of lady's mantle (*Alchemilla mollis*) contribute the gold, and the pale cluster-flowered *Campanula* 'Lodden Anna' blooms softly next to the blossom of the ornamental crab apple. 'Iceberg' roses gleam in the distance.

ABOVE A pretty physic garden in the north of England makes use of London pride (*Saxifraga × urbium primuloides* 'Elliott's Variety') as a dense pink edging. Silvery variegated periwinkle (*Vinca minor* 'Argenteo-variegata') makes a round pool beneath the willow-leaved pear. The yellow flowers of double greater celandine gleam a deeper gold than the foliage of lemon mint in its golden form. In between them lie the large dark leaves of *Salvia sclarea* 'Turkestanica'. Gardeners are surprised by the attractive bed on the left, edged in a white form of thrift, which is filled with the creamy flowers of *Aegopodium podagraria* – ground elder, regarded by gardeners as a pernicious weed, although the variegated form is gaining popularity. In the past it was valued as a spinach-like pot-herb and a remedy for gout.

The creamy blooms on the far side make good plants for present-day gardens. On the left, white comfrey and a huge and frothy meadowsweet, *Filipendula camtschatica*.

OPPOSITE TOP LEFT Part of the Culpepper garden which shows an awareness of colour as well as herbal significance. The belled spires of foxglove in varying shades of rose and pink rise up behind full-flowered paeonies, their handsome but floppy

foliage restrained by a box hedge.

Paeonies make excellent garden plants and will thrive in a fertile soil. Once established, they appreciate some bonemeal and compost lightly worked in every autumn; otherwise, if left undisturbed they will flower for many years.

TOP RIGHT A starry hedge of *Clematis* 'Tetrarose' is for those who prefer prolific dainty blooms to huge

floppy hybrids. 'Tetrarose' is a pink cultivar of *Clematis montana*. Like the species, it is easy-going and will grow well in any fertile soil and any aspect, brightening north-facing walls or hedges. It will scramble vigorously up a tree or bush, but on a wall it is best to train it carefully along wires or a trellis or it will make unsightly knots of tangling foliage. It does not require pruning but may be cut back after flowering.

ABOVE A casual setting made up of deep pinks and golds with a large-flowered everlasting pea *Lathyrus grandiflorus* giving the predominant coloration – dark pink paling towards the flower keels. A completely different shade of pink is provided by the saxifrage, its rosettes of glossy leaves edging out over the path. Variegated periwinkles give additional colour, forming a backdrop to this informal arrangement.

LEFT A neat wall garden of reds and greens, with foliage set against the red brick and terracotta. A few white pot-flowers, petunias and pelargoniums (pot geraniums), line the steps, and there are flecks of cream in the *Euonymus fortunei* 'Silver Queen' inside the box bed, and touches of gold in the box cones at the corners of the square beds. Among the several kinds of gold-tipped box, 'Latifolia Maculata' is one of the most popular. In the handsome pot, the centrepiece of the square holds a fruit tree (probably peach). This pot, too large to be easily moved, could be insulated on very cold nights with sacking or plaited straw.

ABOVE Greens, whites and golds with plenty of foliage variegation set the theme for this small town garden. Raised beds hold climbers, and plants in pots include gold and cream variegated hostas with generous corduroy-textured leaves. Many good hostas have become available recently. 'Gold Standard' and a cream-edged 'Thomas Hogg' are both reliable. The male fern *Dyopteris filixmas*, which obligingly grows in dark corners and almost looks after itself, and the gold-tinted grass *Pleioblastus viridistriatus* (syn.) *Arundinaria*, an ornamental bamboo, add contrasting textures, while a willow-leaved pear makes an unusual standard for a pot.

BELOW A softly informal border in greens, golds and white. To the rear is the white climbing rose *Rosa helenae*, similar to the popular 'Kiftsgate' but not so ferociously rampant, intertwining with *Clematis montana* f. *grandiflora*, which also has white flowers. Linking the climbers with the herbaceous plants is a sturdy clump of pure white *Campanula latifolia*. The grey *Stachys byzantina* (syn.) *S. lanata* picks up the blue and grey tones of other foliage, uniting the group which might otherwise have too harsh an effect.

Orange and yellows are confined to the middle and front of the border, yellow irises (not in flower) in the centre, dwarf iris near the lawn. Butter-coloured pansies gleam brightly next to a doggedly persistent orange wallflower.

Golden lemon balm and generous cushions of golden marjoram make a variegated effect in front of the campanula, while to the left we can just glimpse the bright flash of the foliage of the attractive golden variegated meadowsweet *Filipendula ulmaria* 'Aureo'.

The grey-tinged, iris-like leaves in the front of the border belong to *Sisyrinchium striatum*, which not only flowers but also self-seeds regularly, producing pleasing pale straw-yellow columns of flowers.

RIGHT A rather more formal design of greens, yellows and white, within a patterned framework of box-edged beds and brick paths, is a triumph for designer Arabella Lennox-Boyd. The rectangular bed of yellow flowers is one of four, set symmetrically around the centre bed of white-flowered plants, including the rose 'Moonlight' and the fragrant, white dianthus 'Mrs Sinkins'.

The yellow cluster-flowered floribunda rose 'Norwich Union', particularly recommended as a compact bedding flower, grows at the centre of the yellow bed. The full-petalled blooms fade to a pale lemon, close in colour to the *Helianthemum* 'Wisley Primrose' which grows alongside them. Further along, the ever-popular *Alchemilla mollis* takes up the theme.

Foliage of different textures increases the lush variety of this bed: the gold-edged *Hosta fortunei* 'Aureo-marginata', spear-leaved agapanthus, purple-tinged sage and grey santolina. To the left, the handsome foliage of the Corsican hellebore (*Helleborus argutifolius* syn. *H. corsicus*) is all the more striking against trim box, santolina and lavender.

The fragrant yellow-salmony rose 'Maigold', an early-flowering climber, covers the far pergola, with a yellow day lily at its foot.

THE
SOCIAL GARDEN

A house should lead into the garden in a generous manner – an open invitation to the outdoors. What is more natural and enjoyable than to pad outside on a summer morning to pick a few strawberries or red currants for a family breakfast in the early sunshine, or to sit with friends in the still of an evening watching the creamy beauty of the palest flowers as they seem to float in the twilight of their foliage? Such moments are most precious for those of us who lead busy lives and enjoyable for those of us who live with unpredictable weather and it is important to discover a garden's pleasantest places and adjust the design to make fullest use of them.

There will be select spots which catch the fleeting winter sun and these should be capitalized upon: place a bench near a sunny wall, and grow fragrant winter-flowering shrubs and climbers there, for example. For the summer, there should be a shaded corner, or arbour, where newspapers and correspondence can be read and discussed without the glare of the pages dazzling your eyes.

A terrace near the house makes a pleasant half-way stage between the house and the garden proper, and, if there is adequate shelter from the elements, will be a good place to eat out. Over the last few decades there has been a huge increase in the popularity of eating and cooking outside. Barbecues of varying elaborateness are best-sellers in garden stores but rarely improve the appearance of the garden unless they are designed as an integral part, to merge with the fabric of the rest of the garden. Facilities for children, such as swings, rope ladders, tree houses and sand pits, can also be built invitingly into an overall scheme instead of making an eyesore.

Even swimming pools are being designed in ways more attractive to the garden as a whole, dropped into sunken gardens, girded round with shrubs and flowering plants or reflecting a pretty summerhouse used as a changing room. The breakthrough here has happened with the recognition that pools need not be a startling shade of blue but can blend in greens and browns with the rest of the garden.

The rose 'Albertine' in late summer, when its pink fades to
a pretty creamy blush, intertwined with the cream-white of
'City of York', making an awning over a white bench.
Scented pelargoniums (geraniums), *Akebia*, *Datura*,
kumquat and cactus line this southern aspect in summer,
and go into the conservatory (sun porch) for winter.

Unabashed simple indulgence: coffee and teacakes on the terrace. This is one of the best rooms of the house on warmer days. Pots and troughs supplement the roses, climbers and other plants growing from the narrow beds by the house.

Tiny blooms of apricot-pink dianthus and a delicate small species gladiolus (*Gladiolus communis byzantinus*), early-flowering in dark pink-purple, will soon be followed by the more robust drama of lilies.

Colours do not fight in this garden, thanks to use of darker foliage and variegated ivy to make an interesting background for the flowers. The white flowers of snow-in-summer (*Cerastium*) pick up the white paint of doors and window frames against the grey stone and paving and make a welcome change from the nearly ubiquitous *Alchemilla mollis*.

The owner, a lover of tapestry, has here created a quiet secluded space in which to relax or work. Patterns of light and shade, foliage and flowers, and restrained colour all play their part in creating the total impression of designed simplicity.

A cleverly designed town garden which makes the most of space so that even the children's sandpit is an attractive place both to play in and to look at. It is, nonetheless, partly screened by foliage and large pots from the main sitting area, which is ringed around with metal arches with climbing plants growing over them.

Much use is made of foliage colour and textures in this rather shaded garden – grey helichrysum at the top of the steps and dotted in the flowerbeds, *Choisya ternata* with its glossy, star-shaped foliage, wide-leaved blue-grey hostas and variegated silver and green ivy.

The few flowers in this north-facing garden are mostly pale and luminous: the pots of fuchsia, white impatiens and pink petunias, and towards the back wall nicotiana and Japanese anemone.

The changes of level, the brick-work and planting, framing three separate social areas within a relatively small space, exemplify the way in which the built environment and growing plants can work together to create an integrated whole.

Formal bedding within a very formal framework contributes to an unexpectedly unconventional, almost intimate, effect in this famous topiary garden at Levens Hall in the north of England. The inky, dark foliage of common yew contrasts strikingly with square-clipped golden yew and low box hedging.

The central yew tree is cut into a rounded umbrella shape, and the surrounding bench draws attention to the beautiful flaky red-brown and crimson bark, characteristic of old specimens of common yew.

The shaped beds are thickly planted with creamy-yellow antirrhinums (snapdragons) and mauve verbena (*Verbena venosa*) – annual plants which have been the subject of selective breeding to give a show of flowers all summer long. Amateur gardeners can raise these plants from seed sown early in the year or buy them as small plants.

ABOVE Games and garden furniture can be part of the appeal of a garden. Of all the games possible, croquet and badminton are among the most decorative, and best compatible with a stylish garden.

This scene invites us to participate, either taking up the mallet or – for the less energetic – a seat in the comfortable canvas folding chair, or upon the elegant wrought-iron bench.

The plants, both open-grown and in pots, create an attractive ambiance; foliage shades the seat, rock plants and ivy drape themselves over the retaining wall of local stone.

The terracotta pot holds a great bouquet of fuchsia and the daisy-like *Argyranthemum foeniculaceum*, an attractive plant for container-growing which blooms marvellously all summer long. (You may find it for

sale in garden centres under its old name of *Chrysanthemum foeniculaceum*.)

OPPOSITE TOP In this part of a Cornish garden, with its mild south-western climate, the season begins early and the fresh gold of daffodils appears several weeks before those in gardens elsewhere in Britain. Tall hybrids such as these always look better in beds than naturalized in

grass, where species daffodils or small early hybrids are preferable. Three attractive individual seats pushed together, and secured, look like a lacy bench, catching the early spring sunshine, to make an attractive feature. They stand on paving but the path leading up to them is of slate.

It is a good idea to watch where the sun falls in spring and summer and to design a garden with terraces and paved areas which can benefit most from these unseasonable spells.

It is too early for leaves, but the evergreen makes a screen, and the buds of the young trees and shrubs which surround the seats swell in the bright sunshine.

ABOVE The white, latticework summerhouse sets the tone of this garden planted in whites, greys and creams. A slightly oriental feel is created by the cane furniture and the formal lawn, which mirrors the summerhouse and is planted with the sweet-scented chamomile 'Treneague'.

The two pots contain nicely proportioned standard myrtles (*Myrtus communis*), a Mediterranean native with beautifully scented white flowers and aromatic leaves – but hardy only in warm climates.

ABOVE Cane and wood garden furniture fit well into this mellow autumn scene in Italy. The newly made terrace looks out over walls, made mysterious by a dense shawl of creeper, caught at the point of turning into the autumnal crimson. This garden has an ancient enclosed feel to it, but while the trees and climbing foliage give an impression of natural wildness, the railed terrace makes an effective barrier, preserving a comfortable, civilized, social raft from which to enjoy the scene.

RIGHT Swimming pools don't have to shine a lurid kingfisher blue, which looks unnatural in any context. This small pool is made of green marble, and bordered by white stone, a deliciously cool combination under a hot sun. Dazzling white Versailles tubs, with standard trees, flowers and trailing plants, and a pretty bench provide elegant ornamentation. Pampered swimmers can laze under the graceful leafy curtains of the weeping willow or gaze back to the colourful plants of the garden beyond.

THE
HERB GARDEN

The herb garden on a summer day is as sensually alluring to people as it is to bees and butterflies: the heady tang of chamomile sweetening the air; parsley, which looks and tastes so crisply fresh; warmly aromatic marjoram with the small purple flower clusters that bees love; delicate feathers of aniseed-scented fennel; small-leaved spicy thyme; neat compact bush basil (*Ocinum basilicum minimum*), which evokes the southern Mediterranean with its scent; pennyroyal, reminiscent of traditional mint chews; and bergamot, its slightly more piquant partner with a hint of citrus.

To make a herb garden is to become part of a long and creditable historical tradition. Many of the herbs of the old physic gardens, such as alecost, elecampane or marsh mallow, continue to be grown for their beauty rather than domestic use. More familiar are those which we add to salads or use as flavouring and it is worth noting that the beneficial virtues of most of these herbs have been scientifically accredited.

A comfortably spacious herb garden can include large, statuesque plants such as angelica and lovage, scaling down with bushy fennel, melissa, dill and sage, and the lower humps of santolina (cotton lavender) or cushions of golden marjoram, to the tiny herbs such as the smallest mints and thymes which can snuggle into minute gaps in paving.

There are formal ways of organizing herbs, for example, within a knot pattern of low-growing box hedge or a checker design of paving, but such arrangements need to be skilfully governed. Herbs are naturally anarchic and exuberant in their growth and many of the most interesting herb gardens have a flexible design, allowing for generous growth and self-seeding, while keeping the plants luxuriant and healthy by dividing older ones and growing new stocks from seed every few years.

Some gardeners choose to integrate herbs they use decoratively with other plants into beds and borders. Some grow them purely as ornamental plants.

Herbs don't have to be open grown – bay, santolina and rosemary can be trained as standards into a long-stemmed lollypop shape, or clipped into cones or spirals. A pot or trough of herbs can be unusual and effective in a formal arrangement, while a herb-filled hanging basket is a successful antidote to an overcast summer.

A lush herb garden in Belgium, not far from Brussels, where blue-grey sage is set against purple sage and grey artemisia. A thick mat of golden marjoram contrasts with the clumps of hyssop planted around the sundial as does the free-flowering purple catnip with the neatly clipped box on either side of the Lutyens bench.

ABOVE LEFT An informal herb garden interplanted with roses and other ornamental plants centres on a honey locust tree, *Gleditsia triacanthos*, an unusual subject for a container, but very hardy. This species has ferocious thorns on its attractive cinnamon-coloured trunk, so tamed forms of the golden cultivar 'Sunburst' are the ones usually planted in gardens.

BELOW LEFT A Dutch walled garden, where a soft coloured brick path ends with a terracotta pot of flourishing rosemary. Generously clumpy herbs, chives, and bushy marjoram and feverfew spill over the path, with rue, artemisia and mints making taller shapes.

ABOVE Late summer in this south of England herb garden shows us tall feathery green and bronze fennel, its foliage beginning to fade. Tiny delicious strawberries (probably alpines which have a long fruiting season compared with the wild strawberries of midsummer) are more piquant in taste than the large garden strawberry, and will crop for many years. Between and around the flagstones, heathers are intermingled with herbs: golden feverfew, fennel grown summer-tall, chives and mats of thyme. If space is at a premium, mints and fennels can be cut back when they become tall and gawky and this will bring the benefit of fresh, late-summer foliage.

ABOVE Sun-loving plants grown around a sundial in a garden in the south of England, pink-purple chive flowers contrasting beautifully with the glowing Cotswold stone and a large bush of the rose 'Nevada' in the background.

The chives look good with the silver-grey curry plant (*Heilichrysum angustifolium*) and the deep green of parsley. The characteristic black-purple veining and stem colour of peppermint grows through the greener spearmint, which is more vigorous. Variegated ginger mint and wide-leaved apple mint merge into the bushy blue-green foliage of the artemisia to the right.

RIGHT Whitening this brick wall makes a background which accentuates the rose blooms and foliage in this walled Dutch herb garden, while also lightening the inner garden.

Neat box hedges line the path, and inside the beds, neat bushy clumps of herbs are closely packed without bullying each other. The pinks and purples of lavender, chives, roses and foxglove combine softly, while the different greens and foliage shapes (of basil, tarragon, sorrel and mints) relate to each other to make a subtly patterned effect and a herb garden which is at one time practical, visually attractive and well managed.

THE
FORMAL GARDEN

Formal gardens on a grand scale, such as at Versailles or Hampton Court, or the Dutch palace gardens at Het Loo with their intricately embroidered flowerbed and gravel patterns, give a sense of mastery over unruly Nature. On a smaller scale, they represent a householder's attempt to create a pleasing order within a small space which is continuously attractive.

A formal garden, structured for all-year-round use, is a taxing undertaking for it must contain enough imaginative variation through the seasons for it not to become dull with time. A formal plant effect is generally achieved by use of evergreen. The slow-growing dwarf box, known as *Buxus sempervirens* 'Suffruticosa', is a great resource, out of which one can make knots and patterns as simple or as complicated as one's taste and skill determine.

Ready-made topiary is being introduced from places such as Boskoop in Holland and California, and enterprising manufacturers are providing special frames which place complicated topiary shapes within the grasp of amateurs. Topiary can be made (freehand or with the use of frames) on subjects in pots or tubs, out of hedging, or on the top of a hedge to break the line. One of the most interesting large-scale subjects is a chess game in yew: the one at Brickwall in East Sussex, England, shows a game at the point of the winning move.

A particular feature of the restored seventeenth-century gardens at Het Loo is the way the narrow beds are planted, giving plenty of space to each separate plant. To the present-day gardener, accustomed to the overflowing luxuriance of planting, this comes as a striking change. It works very well within the frame of a formal garden, giving a tulip, a hyacinth, a primrose, a rose or clematis tripod its proper space and dignity, allowing for a full appreciation of the complete form and proportions. It is one of the few outdoor designs which suit hyacinths, and some other statuesque plants such as crown imperials look very well in 'sparse planting' of this kind. Given a weed-free start and a thick bark mulch used in conjunction with a weed-suppressing 'under-blanket' of woven polypropylene, such a scheme is reasonably easy for the modern gardener to achieve and maintain single-handed.

A formal garden does not necessitate an entirely rigid design. A few permanent plants such as well-placed cone-shaped or rounded box-trees or clipped yews, together with walls, statuary and urns, pots or other containers, can create a firm sense of form. Upon this disciplined 'bone structure' a naturalistic summer-flowering scheme can co-exist, offering its owner the joys of luxuriant perennial growth in the summer and a stripped-back formality for the winter.

The beauty of this garden is as apparent in winter as in summer. The four enclosures and the hedges between them with their box-edged symmetry can be seen from an upstairs window. Walking inside it, the garden reveals each part sequentially. An interesting design for a strip of land only 40 × 7 m (132 × 23 ft).

ABOVE A lovely mixture of sunlit honey-coloured Cotswold stone and box. Coloured dabs of orange and red contributed by wallflowers and tulips brighten the narrow beds dominated by two plump box balls. The double cake-stand box with its slurred arch is very ancient, trimmed to shape every year about midsummer. This kind of tiered effect can also be achieved using holly and yew. It entails clearing the trunk of outward-growing branches at intervals and clipping and training the remaining foliage to shape, using a cord as a cutting guide. Box (*Buxus sempervirens*), though slow growing, is one of the most obliging trees for the beginner at topiary.

RIGHT Magnificent magnolias flank this grand doorway with its semi-circular steps leading down to a paved area which has lost some of its formality thanks to outcrops of *Alchemilla mollis*, the spiky-leaved *Sisyrinchium* and blue-green humps of the herb rue. *Magnolia grandiflora* with its dark, glossy evergreen leaves is best grown as a wall shrub since it needs shelter, out of the way of cold north and east winds. Its very beautiful creamy-white fragrant flowers appear in late summer. Matching half-barrels of white petunias and pink-purple fuchsias add touches of extra colour against the impressive backdrop of dark magnolia foliage.

ABOVE England's Hidcote is a garden which drew on French and Italian traditions of formal design and combined them with imaginative and skillful English ideas about planting. One of Britain's most influential gardens, begun by Laurence Johnston soon after he acquired the property in 1909, and gradually augmented until it stood as one of the most important setters of style, it fell into disrepair after World War II, but was restored by the National Trust.

The formal architectural design is everywhere modified by the luxuriance and taste of the planting in a style which has since become the hallmark of English gardening. The ten acres of the estate are subdivided into a series of intimate inner gardens, each with its own separate character, divided by walls and hedges.

The hedging plants at Hidcote are numbered in thousands, the picture above showing generous sculpting of box which dissolves into low box hedging, in this case the clipped

species *Buxus sempervirens* (the cultivar 'Suffruticosa' with smaller leaves is sometimes preferred for very low hedging), but here the the line flows generously from the rounded shapes to the knee-high hedge.

TOP RIGHT A cool *allée* in a Dutch garden with high beech hedges each side and plants which tolerate shade: box balls and a small-leaved type of glossy bergenia densely cover every patch of soil in the two borders.

ABOVE RIGHT A section of the purely ornamental gardens at the château of Villandry on the Loire to the east of Tours. From an upper terrace, you can see the role it plays in a formal pattern of gardens edged in box with yew sentries clipped into four tiers. A bed of densely planted glowing *Rudbeckia* lies behind the tiered clipped yew, while a tall, thick hornbeam hedge separates the garden from the lime trees which enclose the area beyond.

FAR LEFT A dainty summerhouse and a stone font make the focal point for this formal white garden in South Island, New Zealand, with its geometry of narrow brick paths enclosing brick-edged beds. The patterning of the brick, together with the evergreen box, is neat for the winter, though in summer the plants are allowed to break with strict formality. The rose 'Wedding Day' grows over the pergola and the cultivar *Rosa rugosa* 'Blanc Double de Coubert' masses gracefully in the flowerbeds, with phlox, dahlias and white gladioli as supporting cast. The owner also grows astilbe and a number of variegated and silver-leaved plants.

ABOVE LEFT Terracotta pots, reddish-blue brick, and box and herbaceous plants make a mosaic of textures, against which pale flowers gleam brilliantly. This Belgian garden is a combination of formality and generous planting, of old-fashioned and good modern plants.

The large pot of *Convolvulus cneorum*, with its dainty pink buds and silvered foliage, makes a good centrepiece. Forming fragrant bushes on either side of the elegant Lutyens bench is the rose 'Stanwell Perpetual', one of the owner's particular favourites, 'for its fern-like, grey-green leaves and pale pink blooms which last all summer through'. The small-leaved clematis species with dainty, nodding purple flowers, *Clematis viticella*, climbs over the arch.

BELOW LEFT A tall, evergreen yew hedge is made into an alcove to accommodate a bench of delicate tracery. Low formal beds edged neatly in box are dominated by the corduroy-textured leaves of hostas and blur attractively with other plants in the dappled shade.

ABOVE Formality can be achieved in
a grass walk rather than the usual
brick or stone. The design of this
Italian garden, at Tyninghame in
south-east Scotland, is held together
by the symmetry of the yew hedges
and climber-covered arches and
thoughtful planting. Border edges of
catnip (*Nepeta × faassenii*) spill over the
grass and make a pink-purple cloud
behind the winged bronze statue,
viewed through the final arch
supporting the rose 'Zéphirine
Drouhin' in full flower and a vigorous
grape vine.

RIGHT A beautifully designed herb
garden in the south of England, with
formal box-edged beds and a thriving
association of choice and unusual
plants. The beds and the narrow brick
paths between them meet in eight
points at an armillary sphere on an
ornamented pedestal. *Astrantia,
Polemonium*, lilies, roses, and irises
grow alongside some of the more
familiar kitchen herbs, such as
variegated salvias, borage and mints.
Roses on supports add height, and
clematis and roses in matching yellow
drape the wall behind.

THE HOT-CLIMATE GARDEN

Gardening under an unrelenting sun one quickly learns the sweet virtue of shade; in the strong, hard, penetrating light the brilliant, hot colours of the flowers make their gaudy assault. More gradually, the relationships between the nature of the plants and their environment reveal themselves: drought survivors such as cacti and the agave family defend themselves from predation with spines, needles, razor-sharp leaves or spikes; fruit and flowers are adapted to minutely specific pollinating insects.

To people living in temperate zones, the complete experience of hot-climate gardens is glimpsed only on vacation, but in fact many hot-climate plants adapt surprisingly well to a change of conditions. A few parts of England are both hot and dry, a fact exploited by Beth Chatto in her garden near Colchester in East Anglia. On ground so barren that common weeds died, she designed a Mediterranean garden of drought-resistant plants which thrived colourfully.

Many of the earliest garden plants in western culture were brought from the Mediterranean and later, after the Crusades, from Turkey and the rest of Asia Minor. The rich flora of southern Africa has been a plentiful source of garden plants, as have India and the Himalayas, the Americas and China. More recently New Zealand and Australian flora have been explored, not simply the hebes and the eucalyptuses but also a range of trees, shrubs, bulbs and other herbaceous plants.

These hot-climate plants will grow in warmer, drier parts of temperate countries, against warm walls, and on sloping banks. Many of them are perennials which have to be discarded after they have flowered once because they will not survive the winter, though this can be avoided if they are nurtured as pot plants and overwintered in sheltered conditions. Cacti, poinsettias and daturas never reach the size they would in their natural conditions but they will survive in conditions quite alien to them.

Whether this is quite fair to the plant is a matter for individual conscience, and there is considerable doubt about the legitimacy of a number of plant imports from the wild. There are, however, plants which have been bred over the centuries for use in cooler gardens and we now have an array of home-bred lilies and house-trained orchids, tulip cultivars numbered in the thousands, and many others which are as cherished as old friends.

A garden in the Alpes Maritimes in south-eastern France: low box snakes around orange trees grown as half-standards and fragrant myrtle in terracotta pots. This photograph was taken before an unusually savage frost swept the area, doing considerable damage.

TOP A superb location for a house, looking over Grasse to the hills beyond in the south of France, the view punctuated by the tall needles of juniper trees. Pale-flowered oleanders are just beginning to come into bloom, and a spreading palm gives a little shade to the pool.

ABOVE You can almost smell the sea air of Sydney Harbour. There is no soft mistiness here. Everything is crisply delineated in the clear, bright light: the gleaming pillars, the plant pots – even the separate leaves of the clipped variegated holly, the small daisy-like flowers and the floppy white heat-struck petals.

RIGHT An old donkey path in the Algarve in Portugal, leading to two water tanks, part of an ancient Arabic irrigation system, has been fashioned into a shade-giving rose pergola. Though the water system still functions, donkeys no longer walk this worn cobbled path, lined with green foliage in the shade, giving on to greys in the sunshine beyond.

The rose 'Bella Portuguesa' was raised in Portugal about the turn of the century. A good climbing rose, it flowers abundantly, its blooms pink with darker shading. Available as 'Belle Portugaise' and 'Belle of Portugal', it requires a warm sheltered position to do well.

ABOVE A beautifully elegant display of luxuriant clipped cherry laurels in weathered old Anduze pots. They could hardly be shown to better advantage than against this plain wall of an old building in Provence, but by the same token, they have to be in absolutely perfect condition, for any flaw is equally exposed.

Ideally, laurels should be hand-clipped with care taken not to sever individual leaves, but nobody has the help to manage that nowadays, and pot-grown specimens can look this good if kept fertile and well watered and clipped carefully by machine.

RIGHT An irresistible Provençal garden, La Chèvre d'Or on the Côte d'Azur, formally designed but bursting with *joie de vivre*. The exuberance of the surrounding woodland endows the classic valley garden with a sense of quiet repose.

This is a very sensual garden: the sound of water from the simple fountain in the shallow green pool, the ripe oranges on the trees, the crisp texture of the ingenious box hedges against the velvet grass, the dark evergreens contrasting with the flowering pale lilac plumes of the open-grown wisteria and grey olives and eucalyptus in the distance. Old and invitingly worn steps lead from the bank down to the pool – it all makes one want to surrender completely to one's senses and drink in every aspect of the beauty.

ABOVE The idea for the 'Judas tree walk' at this beautiful garden in Provence was suggested to the owner, the Vicomte de Noailles, by an English landscape gardener.

Indeed this elegant, witty garden tucked into a limestone cliff, with its groves and terraces, fountains and pools, owes many of its ideas to his library of English garden writers as well as to observations made during a long lifetime of visiting gardens, enjoying the arts and making a study of botany and garden plants.

Charles de Noailles wished to 'create a quiet garden without extravagant effects or grand vistas, which would bring pleasure to the inhabitants of the house and visitors'.

The Judas tree *Cercis siliquastrum*, widely introduced elsewhere because of its strange beauty, is native to the Mediterranean. The *alleé* of Judas trees, about 45 m (148 ft) long, was designed by the vicomte to lead from the house to the wild cyclamen garden. In April when the deep pink laburnum-like flowers come into bloom (before the leaves appear), it is a tunnel of flower, informally paved with limestone and dotted about with daisies, buttercups, bluebells and other wild flowers.

ABOVE A fresh, early summer day in a part of Provence which turns hot, dry and parched later in the season. The small vineyard is bordered with a pretty flower walk. The lower part is confined to roses; the nearer is a mixture, with foxgloves in the ascendant at this point. Bearded irises make an attractive group at the place where the grass path leads out through the vines. There are also clumps of fragrant pinks, plants which do well in this climate; several kinds grow wild beyond the garden gates (proving this point).

The climate is one of extremes, a cold hard winter, which gives way to a gentle and beautiful spring, followed by a scorching summer. However this may seem to human beings, there are many plants which thrive in it, and the Mediterranean basin and the adjoining regions are a honey-pot for garden visitors and botanists alike.

Small vineyards such as this one are a common sight in this region, near Les Alpilles, and the rows of neatly pruned-back vines, integrated within small fields or incorporated with gardens, are much more picturesque than huge vineyards stretching over several acres.

THE
SECRET GARDEN

The allure of Frances Hodgson Burnett's book *The Secret Garden*, extending far beyond its literary qualities, has caused many of us to grow up with a desire for a hidden garden – private, secluded, beautiful and overgrown, sheltering and enclosing us, making us feel immune from the upheavals of the world outside. Inside it, flowers bloom, birds sing and there is fragrance in the air. It is a powerful theme in literature, from the Garden of Eden to the Madonna's garden, the *hortus conclusus* of medieval times, the *giardino segreto* of the Italian Renaissance, and beyond.

In modern times, secret, romantic gardens enable us to cut ourselves off physically from our everyday lives and business and afford our minds and souls a period of quiet relaxation and reflection. Perhaps this is why so many town gardens are unexpected gems – exhibiting a variety of styles and fulfilling an important psychological purpose.

Water, whether a diverting trickle, fountain or still pool, helps to compose the romantic mood. Fragrance – some roses over a pergola or growing through a tree – and cascades of flowers such as *Wisteria floribunda* 'Alba' contribute to the effect. A fruit tunnel or pergola might be added for a more sophisticated taste or a quiet arbour of golden hops or scented clematis varieties. For those who favour wilder romance, a fallen trunk overgrown with flowers and ferns or a tree growing aslant might be sought.

A hidden courtyard, a paved area close to the house, can be designed for complete seclusion. It must not be left to its own devices but gently gardened to encourage plants between the paving: a few herbs perhaps, yellow corydalis and *Alchemilla mollis* which love crevices and crannies, but also some taller plants such as foxgloves or an elegant ornamental grass. Finally, add the human element to the scene, clad, ideally, in a straw boater and softly flowing garments. All must be viewed slightly out of focus – it helps if you are short-sighted.

A scented arcade of foliage-covered arches, thickly underplanted, the outlines of the paving softly edged in green. The framing arch supports honeysuckle and clematis; beyond, there are roses and other climbers. Thymes, pansies, violas and other plants blur softly below.

LEFT Oriental poppies with a pink and coral colour which goes very well with their grey-green leaves, grouped outside an enclosed *potager*, rather medieval in character, of brick topped with trellis. Outside with the poppies we glimpse a heavily laden standard gooseberry, within a surround of strawberries or perhaps some other round-leaved plant, protected by a narrow box circlet. There is golden marjoram and mint, hyssop and other plants which are indistinct from this distance. The little garden within a garden keeps its secrets.

ABOVE A view designed to maximize the drama of the transition from dark to light, as one peers through the yew arch into the bright seclusion of a garden hedged with tall yew.

The bench on the far side is placed so one can sit quietly and reflect, or simply enjoy the sight and scents of the garden. It is quite densely planted, with spring- and summer-flowering plants and evergreens providing something of interest for most times of the year. The most arresting plants of early summer are the roses and bearded irises.

TOP Behind a small terraced cottage a tiny white garden hedged, and densely planted, looks natural and flowing but is in actuality a model of ingenuity and restraint. No plant is allowed to jostle or bully its neighbours. *Leucanthemum* × *superbum* 'H. Siebert' and a double campanula make a blaze of white; opposite, striped leaves of *Iris pallida* mingle with an unusual pink-flowered *Campanula punctata*. Spirea glimmers dark pink behind the blue *Clematis* × *durandii* and the rose 'Pink Garnet' glows brightly by the box hedge, while a daisy bloom of *Anthemis cretica* subsp. *cupaniana* rises from dainty greyish foliage in the urn.

ABOVE The Corona at Athelhampton in Dorset, England, is the centrepoint of this intimate, many-chambered garden. Red dahlias, lilies, eucalyptus, fuchsias, Solomon's seal and abutilon enjoy the shelter of the stone circle but never obscure its profile.

RIGHT Looking under the arch adorned with the climbing rose 'Leverhusen', we find a shady garden with tree paeony, *Geranium endressi* and roses. The white rose on the tiled shed is a unique seedling of 'Kiftsgate' spotted by Mr Humphrey Brooke and named 'Limekiln' after his beautiful rose garden.

An archway through a wall of lichen-dotted local stone, in an Oxfordshire garden in England, covered by a large and flowery rose, 'Albertine', frames a view to an inner garden. The semi-evergreen honeysuckle *Lonicera sempervirens* grows close to the archway. This species looks glamorous but, disappointingly, it does not have the honeysuckle fragrance. Two large mounds of grey-foliaged cotton lavender, *Santolina chamaecyparissus*, hug the ground on either side. The plant is grown for both its pretty grey foliage

and the pleasant scent of its leaves when crushed or pressed.

The view within shows a low box hedge surrounding a central Victorian urn which is standing amidst a fragrant chamomile lawn, backed by a great surge of pink and white roses.

The arch and the glimpse of the garden within a garden has the effect of enlivening the scene and making both inner and outer regions seem more interesting because of the way the eye deals with the double perspective. Even in a small garden an archway can play tricks with a vista.

A flowery garden corner framed by a drystone wall makes a pleasantly out-of-the-way place to have a few private moments with a book or a letter. The subtle, pale-green cups of the hellebore grow through the ends of the plain and romantically dilapidated seat while the area is lit up with the clear orange flowers of the Welsh poppy *Meconopsis cambrica*. This poppy is a perennial which tends to be short-lived, but it seeds freely and once you have established it you generally have a friend for life. There is a pretty clear-yellow form too.

Close to the seat the star-like, soft foliage of *Alchemilla mollis* makes a fresh summer cushion, and a gentle green against which the frills of the red paeony show to advantage. After high summer the alchemilla's leaves may get ragged, but if cut back will grow anew. The poppies will continue flowering until almost autumn, and do well in any soil and any position, even a shady corner such as this, beneath the canopy of a gnarled rose, up which a large-flowered purple clematis of the Jackmannii type winds its way.

161

ABOVE LEFT The low light of a late summer makes a quiet glow in this enclosed garden, where the focal point is a curious oval table on a wide-based pedestal. The attractive long bench against the wall is sturdily made with arms and a slatted back, and the one opposite has been kept simple and unpainted so as not to obscure the impression of the scene as a whole.

A scramble of climbing plants clothes the wall (the one on the right looks like a *Vitis coignetiae* just beginning to change colour). The scented-leaf pelargoniums (geraniums) on the table can be rubbed contemplatively by anyone sitting on the bench in order to release their fragrance; those in the corner will be brushed by anyone going past, with the same result.

These pelargoniums make excellent and very attractive pot plants, growing well without excessive watering or feeding, and thriving outdoors until the first frosts arrive. There are several kinds, almost all of which are suitable for pots. The familiar lemon pelargonium (*P. graveolens*) is perhaps the easiest to look after and its leaves can be used in cooking. (It has an upright variegated form.) *Pelargonium* × *fragrans*, which has beautiful soft, small grey-green leaves, has a gently resiny scent, not so

strong as the pungent *P. quercifolium*. Another good species is *Pelargonium tomentosum*, which has large velvety leaves that smell deliciously of peppermint, but is more susceptible to cold than the others.

ABOVE RIGHT An unusual and very private garden in Haarlem, Holland, with a stylishly simple bench and table backed by a screen of freshly cut young poles. Ivy is growing behind the screen, a feature in itself, so the plants get no encouragement to climb up and cover it in a glossy evergreen drapery.

To match this spare simplicity, the paved area is plainly but beautifully laid in neat small bricks and larger textured flagstones, making a crisply contrasting hard island within the surrounding plants.

The vegetation consists of subdued greens and blues. The narrow foliage of *Tradescantia* × *andersoniana* makes a kind of dark glossy thatch out of which the purplish blue three-petalled flowers gleam like small stars.

The pale lavender bells of the bellflower *Campanula carpatica* glimmer softly, looking more fragile than they are. Most campanulas will grow equally well in sun or partial shade, but it was a surprise to see the sedum (*Sedum spectabile*), which generally requires full sun, in this rather shaded garden.

A remarkable compartment consisting of a 2 m (6½ ft) hornbeam hedge planted in a strictly precise rectangle, with an inner planting of quince trees on the long sides.

In autumn the effect is a brown harvest glow, the quince leaves littering the ground ornamentally. In spring, both trees bring out their young leaves rather early; the hornbeams are a rich mid-green, each one pleated, as if it had been carefully folded so as to fit inside the bud. Quince leaves appear almost white, luminously powdery-pale in the spring sun.

They are still pale when they are fully open but darken as the season progresses, and palest pink flowers like scentless roses appear along the branches. During this period the hornbeam is thick, green and dense but the foliage begins to thin as autumn nears. The quince fruits become ripe in early autumn, curiously shaped golden oblongs with an unmistakable, tangy, spicy smell, unlike any other fruit.

The winter garden is a tangle of branches, the grey trunks of the hornbeam striated as if they had overstretched their early growth, the branches of the quince a happy muddle, the twig tips of the small avenue meeting in the centre.

THE
CONTAINER GARDEN

Container gardening opens up new opportunities. Apartment dwellers and the gardenless sometimes forget is that even grand gardeners with limitless domains use container plants for special effects. But, as in all gardening, there is art and skill in what you grow and the way you arrange it. It is not good enough to find a reasonably nice container – window box, tub, pot, urn or hanging basket – and stuff it with plants. Without considering the shape of the containers, the material of which they are made, where they are to be situated and the context in which they are to be seen, it is all too easy to end up with a haphazard and untidy display.

There is hardly anything which cannot be grown in a pot – including trees and shrubs. As for the containers, there are people who cannot resist a good pot or jar and build up splendid collections of these delectable artefacts, picking them up over the years in all kinds of out-of-the-way places. For a specific purpose, however, it is probably best to have some idea of what you are after in your mind's eye (and a few figures relating to shape and space in your head) or you may end up with something completely out of place. Terracotta is a lovely material but poor quality pots flake and crack if subject to frost, especially if they are large ones. Urns are attractive and the best ones are made of real stone; if not, stoneware is often a nicer material than reconstituted stone, which looks pocked. Lead tanks and urns also look good but are fiendishly expensive. A wooden container, such as a barrel, box or trough, is perfectly fine if it is well designed and made (though it must be treated with plant-friendly preservative, not creosote).

Container planting makes possible the use of tender plants, especially if a greenhouse, conservatory or even frost-free garage can be used to protect them in the colder months. With winter shelter, you can countenance lemon verbena, morning glory, *Rhodochiton* with its strange purple umbrellas, and citrus trees. Containers which must stay out of doors all the time can be separately planted for winter and summer, or have a permanent colony of staple plants to which seasonal extras are added. Perennial candytuft, variegated small-leaved ivy, or euonymus such as 'Emerald Gaiety' will stand the winter (unless it is cold enough for the soil to freeze solid) and can be interplanted with bulbs and summer annuals. For simple *joie de vivre* there can be nothing to beat a thickly planted container of trailing ivy-leaved pelargoniums (pot geraniums).

An Italian terracotta pot with an immensely pretty planting
of pelargonium (pot geraniums) and silver-leaved artemisia.
The lovely pelargonium overlapping the top of the pot,
its white flowers with crimson veins at the throat, the
ivy-shaped leaves edged ivory white, is a distinctive
Victorian variety called 'L'Elegante' once again in fashion.

LEFT A beautiful hydrangea (above left) in soft pink makes a flourishing pot plant. *Hydrangea macrophylla* (this one looks like 'Madame Emile Mouillière') thrives in sun or semi-shade but needs rich, moist soil.

A number of palms are grown for their foliage. The young plant (below centre) is probably *Phoenix canariensis*, a plant grown for its dense crown of arching feathery leaves.

Some people like to place individual pots in groups (below right), but it has to be skillfully done or it simply looks untidy. The luxuriantly flowering pot (below left) is designed to look good against the fence and tiles, an ensemble made from plants all commonly available and easy to grow. Behind the mauve petunia is *Argyranthemum frutescens* (formerly *Chrysanthemum frutescens*), while lobelia and *Helichrysum petiolare* drip over the side.

ABOVE A superb arrangement of violet and cerise 'de Caen' anemones beneath a clipped baytree.

TOP A striking purple-planted window box. The theme is set by the bold, dark-leaved *Tradescantia pallida* 'Purpurea' against the white wall and pales through the petunia and lobelia to the bouquet of flowery mauve *Campanula isophylla*, interplanted with red and white pelargoniums and white alyssum.

ABOVE A decorated lead urn spilling over with a deliciously untidy combination of flowers and foliage, typically used in container planting: white petunias, *Helichrysum petiolare*

with *Argyranthemum frutescens* and the intricate, felty foliage of scented-leaf pelargonium. Part of the success of this fountain of bloom is due to its impact against the velvety dark background of the yew hedge.

RIGHT An Italian window box in terracotta, ornamented with swags of fruit. The characteristic elements, pelargoniums, petunias and lobelia, are lit up by the sun against the dark frame of the window, and the bright glossy foliage of Virginia creeper growing around the window.

FAR LEFT An unusual and very effective colour combination lit up by the bright yellow stars of the plant *Bidens ferulifolia*. The familiar shapes of white petunias and *Argyranthemum frutescens* play their parts, dependably as always, the first giving the benefit of larger flowers, the latter height and a link between the white and yellow. Winding through the flowers is the greenish-grey form of *Helichrysum petiolare* 'Limelight', the whole making a spectacular display.

ABOVE LEFT Two exceptionally neat window boxes hanging below windows in a house in Stonington in south-east Connecticut. Clearly designed to catch the eye from a distance with their hard, bright colours, these matching boxes are dominated by large, strong red pelargoniums, with variegated periwinkle (*Vinca major* 'Elegantissima') trailing over the front of the boxes. Among the other bright occupants are marigolds, silver-leaved cineraria (dusty miller) and coleus with green-edged crimson leaves.

BELOW LEFT A pretty informal group of plants with flowers and foliage intermingling. The silver-grey *Artemisia arborescens* makes a light background against which Madonna lilies and variegated grass, gardener's garters (*Phalaris arundinacea* 'Picta'), *Argyranthemum* and a pelargonium with cream-margined leaves are grouped. They make a strong, cool effect in a shady town garden in London. The pot is not terracotta but a plastic copy, very useful for people gardening on roofs or structures where weight is a problem.

THE
FRUIT GARDEN

It used to be taken for granted that fruit was an integral part of any good garden or small estate. The frontispiece for the book *A Gentleman's Recreation,* published in Britain in 1716, shows a small town-house garden with fruit climbing over the house, fan-trees pinned out against the walls and a woman and child and at some distance two gentlemen in discussion on a central path which leads through a formal planting of fruit bushes in turf. For property owners of the seventeenth and eighteenth centuries, growing fruit was not a mundane practicality but a recreational pursuit involving sensual and intellectual pleasure and opportunity for contemplation.

There has been a revival of interest in the fruits of the past. People have realized how beautiful and interesting compact trees such as medlar and quince can be in a small garden. Espaliers and small fruit trees on dwarf stocks are now much more frequently used as decorative living screens, separating one part of a garden from another with foliage, blossom and fruit. Cool walls provide a support for fan-trained morello cherry trees or 'Victoria' plums. Sunny walls have tender plums and sweet cherries, easily protected from the depredations of birds by a simple net cover, much more pleasant than an ugly fruit cage.

Fruits themselves are ornamental: strawberries; red, white and black currants; gooseberries on tall stems or as dense bushes; screens of raspberries; fruit trees trained as 'pyramids', 'goblets' or in the densely bushy head-high form known as *en quenouilles*. With new kinds of rootstocks, it is even possible to grow a sweet cherry in a tub, and a range of fruits may be raised in pots for courtyard or patio ornament. Yet the attention is not entirely on artificially produced shapes and forms, but also on conserving and planting orchards. Even a small patch of ground can support a few small trees, and a standard-sized tree can be planted in a calm corner or by a hedge – so people can again enjoy something of the unique pleasures of the orchard. William Lawson, who gardened in the early seventeenth century, wrote that simply walking through an orchard is the best relaxation for a mind wearied by the work of the day. 'Unspeakable pleasure and infinite commodity,' he tells us, are the rewards of growing fruit trees – raising an orchard is a joy for the present and a pledge to the future.

An apple orchard in full blossom is one of the loveliest sights on earth. This one has been neatened by mowing and forms part of a complete scene which includes a white drift of narcissi, and some formal steps up to the orchard with its classic bench and Versailles tubs.

ABOVE Trained forms of apples bearing their crop. The eye of the camera puts everything into one plane so it is difficult to see clearly how these apples are shaped. The bough on the left, which is curved over, demonstrates the principle which is employed in the 'festoon' shape. This method of growing small fruit trees entails bending over each branch to cause fruit buds to shoot.

The final result gives a tree like a small fountain, a restricted but productive shape for a small or an ornamental kitchen garden.

The principle of festooning can be applied to fruit trees which have a lot of upright growth but are not producing much fruit. The lower branches are bent down in late summer and secured to the trunk or to another branch. The lower branches should be started into making fruit buds and the upper ones should be checked.

RIGHT This garden is ornamental without containing flowers, its decorative effect deriving from neat groupings of fruit and vegetables.

There are ripe broad beans, mature lettuces and carrots, and, before the slender fruit tree, three aubergines (eggplants) about to flower.

Red currant is one of the most attractive fruit bushes and especially so when grown as a standard or a long leg as here. Red currants usually crop quite heavily and the fruit, if left on the plant, will last in a fresh condition for quite a long time. But if birds visiting your garden have developed a taste for red currants, this is irrelevant, unless the fruit is protected by a fruit cage or netting.

LEFT It is only in the more southerly latitudes in Italy, Portugal and Spain. that citrus fruits are able to grow outside in open ground all the year round. Even in a garden in the south of France they are grown in pots (some of which are an ornament in themselves) which are brought into shelter for the winter.

This practice can be carried out further north and many of the old estates in Britain have fruiting citrus trees of a great age. At Saltram House in Devon the citrus fruits are taken under cover in October on the day of the local Goose Fair and put outside again on Oak Apple Day at the end of May.

The elaborate and elegant winter buildings (the forerunners of conservatories or sun spaces) came to be called 'orangeries' after the fruit they housed, and in some countries they were used as theatres for concerts and other entertainments.

TOP The beautiful lemons make marvelous ornamentation for an Italian courtyard, also producing a useful crop of fruit.

ABOVE Ripe grapes as autumn approaches and the large leaves of the vine begin to redden. Although some grape varieties do better in a warm climate, there are a number which will tolerate fairly cool conditions and cold winters. Here the vine is growing outside and, to judge by the compact clusters of small black grapes, it is 'Brandt', a very robust variety. It will quickly cover large walls and buildings, and is often grown purely for ornament, but it seems a shame to ignore its harvest of small sweet grapes.

BELOW Dessert gooseberries are a much under-rated fruit, delicious in summer fruits salads. There are many varieties, which, if left to ripen, turn to green, or to red or white.

Growing a standard gooseberry tree is both very decorative and easier on one's back when picking. Training the tree involves regularly taking off all the lower branches while encouraging a shapely top.

Gooseberries produce lots of fruit, but to get good dessert berries you thin the branches of unripe fruit (for pies) leaving the rest to swell over the next few weeks. Dessert gooseberries not only taste delicious but contain essential fatty acids and are extremely good for you.

RIGHT A small morello cherry tree grown as a fan on a wall. This kind of cherry, with its deliciously tangy sour taste, is less troubled by birds than sweet cherries, and its blooms are rarely afflicted by frost since it is one of the latest to flower. However, many gardeners choose to grow it on walls because it is one of the few fruits which will do well on a north-facing wall ('Victoria' plum is another). It is, however, very vigorous, but if you have a wall which is at least 2 m (6½ ft) high and two to three times as wide, a morello is a beautiful plant to grow. When it is grown in the open, it makes a large well-shaped handsome tree.

THE
PAVED GARDEN

The story of the blind Roman emperor who walked his newest paved roads without shoes to check that the workmanship was up to standard is probably apocryphal but it embodies important principles. First, that you cannot take too much care with paving; second, that there are few nicer things than the feel of well-laid sun-warmed brick or stone under bare feet.

Paving should be a carefully planned part of the garden; it is, after all, one of the most enduring elements. It is always worthwhile using the very best materials, spending as much as you can possibly afford. But even if you select expensive stone or brick, bring a sample home before you make the final choice and check that its colour and texture suit your garden and blend well with the surroundings and the material of which the house is built. Reconstituted stone is very much cheaper than the real thing but never looks as nice and does not wear attractively. Its appearance can be enhanced if the paving is interspersed with two or three brick courses, which gives it a more varied look.

Combinations and patterns used when laying a paved brick or cobbled area can make for a variety of pleasing effects. It is well worth looking at as many different examples as possible before making any decisions. Engineering bricks are often recommended for well-used garden paths, but they give a slightly shiny, hard-edged finish. While ordinary house-bricks will crumble and turn to rubble after continued frost, there are other strong bricks with cut surfaces which are fairly weather-resistant and will serve you at reasonable cost. Grey stable bricks, which are patterned like slab chocolate, are very pleasant, but like granite or grey stone they require another texture or colour to go alongside them to lighten the effect.

Some designers have their paving hallmarks – the Jekyll-Lutyens partnership, for example, created a number of attractive models: lovely wide semi-circular steps with flowers growing from the crevices, curving paths of brick and stone, and areas made from tiles set on their sides. Some of the nicest results are created by laying stone or brick into grass as large areas of stepping stones, although this is not for pathways which can expect a heavy traffic of feet. Modern herb gardens and bulb displays make use of a checker-board effect of small beds set within paving. This provides a good foil for individual plants and prevents invasive plants, such as mints, from spreading.

Narrow beds or borders can be set alongside paving so that flowers and foliage soften its lines, and pots and urns filled with plants can also be used to good effect, especially when the undecorated path is very severe. For those of disciplined tastes, box edging, a pleached avenue of trees, or pots of clipped box, bay or shrubs trained as standards make for a trim formality.

The neatly laid patterns of red brick make a striking framework for the surrounding flowerbeds, symmetrically ordered around a sundial planted round with several kinds of thyme. The dark greens of foliage contrast well with the strong colour of the brick, under the hard light of an Australian sun, the effect softened by greys.

ABOVE A courtyard dining place in a Dutch garden contrived within the old moat (long since disused and dry) which surrounds the house. It has been paved in a lovely pink-red brick which looks well with the ornamental terracotta pots.

A formal element is provided by the box spirals but other plants are trained on the walls and sprawl informally from narrow beds edging the area. A few have been allowed to colonize spaces between the paving, which makes a pretty effect, so long as they do not get out of hand and start pushing the bricks aside.

If you lay your bricks on sand and brush sand (or sand, peat and seed) into the joints, plants soon grow in the interstices. Weeds and overlarge plants should be removed annually and the paved area cleaned.

Some of the pots are filled each spring with annual plants which flower all summer. *Felicia amelloides* has blue daisy-like flowers and slightly fleshy dark green (or variegated) leaves. *Felicia bergeriana* makes a mat of grey, hairy leaves and steely-blue flowers with yellow centres.

Shaped box, trained and clipped in Holland (principally in Boskoop), is now reaching gardeners all over the world at reasonable prices, but with patience, it is possible to do it for yourself within a few years.

To make a spiral like those in the garden above, you first trim the box to a cone shape. Then, tying a piece of string at the top and winding it down in a slow spiral, you begin clipping (from the bottom up) following the string guide. The leaves and stems down to the central trunk should be removed. Alternatively a pliable young tree, wound around a bamboo and tied into place, will eventually hold its spiral shape.

TOP RIGHT The silver-grey garden designed by Gertrude Jekyll for the garden at Hestercombe in Somerset, which enjoys the mild climate of south-west England. The first place to be completely designed by the famous partnership between the architect Sir Edwin Lutyens (who made imaginative use of paving materials, using local stone, cobbles, tiles and flint) and designer and plantswoman Gertrude Jekyll, this important garden has now been restored. The plants used here include *Stachys*, catnip (*Nepeta*), lavenders, cotton lavender (santolina) and hostas.

ABOVE RIGHT An attractive cushion-effect created with the purple of the bell-flower *Campanula portenschlagiana* against the shallow lichened stone steps. This bellflower is hardy, but it requires weeding and feeding to flower attractively.

LEFT A beautiful cloistered garden paved with small bricks and cobblestones, threaded with moss. The light, filtered through a large walnut tree, catches the white of the bench, table roses and a pot of *Argyranthemum frutescens* (formerly *Chrysanthemum frutescens*). Among herbs in the bed near the yew hedge are *Achillea* and sweet Cicely, with their pale flat flowerheads, and feathered fennel. Other white flowers nestle among the shades of green.

The rounded tumps of clipped box in a semi-circle around the statue contrast with the ebullience of the herbs. Small paths radiate between the herbs, which all have white flowers (such as horseradish) or white forms (*Rosmarinus officinalis* 'Albus').

ABOVE A quiet shaded place paved with York stone demonstrating the effect of foliage against stone in a shady area. The owners have chosen a variety of plants with pale green or variegated golden foliage: the gold form of the cut-leaved elder merges with golden hop, with the fronds of lady fern arching over the starry mauve campanula.

To the right of the picture the very dark green of a crimp-leaved form of ivy, called 'Parsley Crested', shines glossily behind the two terracotta pots of fern *Polystichum setiferum* placed between two hostas – a cream-edged variety and (in the bed behind, below the single arch of Solomon's seal) one with foliage touched with creamy yellow on the margin.

ABOVE LEFT The gardenia grown as a standard in a pot was photographed in a garden in Melbourne in south-eastern Australia. It is not an easy plant to grow, but is worth perseverance for the wonderful scent. The 'ball' and the pot match each other for shape, and echo the rich red colour of the path and the high wall draped with ivy and clematis. The bricks are cleverly laid in a pattern with three bricks one way and two at 90 degrees, until two courses before the edge of the steps.

ABOVE RIGHT Two neat little box hedges line this path made from grey stable bricks opening into a circle brightened by yellow pansies around a large pot. This container is full of the wallflower-like Erysimum 'Bowles Mauve', which has silver-grey foliage and richly coloured flowers with just

a trace of scent. It is perennial, though not always hardy in cold winters, and older plants get rather large, so for a container it is best to plant anew every year or so (taking cuttings in late summer).

RIGHT Unequally sized stone flags with spaces left between them for plants: Alchemilla mollis (lady's mantle), its flowers persuaded to spread in a yellow-green halo around the pretty leaves; a bright red mimulus called 'Whitecroft Scarlet'; Campanula poscharskyana; and hostas. These are golden-leaved Hosta fortunei 'Aurea' (next to the mimulus); Hosta fortunei 'Albopicta', the golden one with the darker green margins; 'Frances Williams' to the fore with the yellow margins; and Hosta undulata with the bold ivory slash down the centres of the leaves.

INDEX OF PLANTS

ACKNOWLEDGMENTS

The publisher thanks the following photographers and organizations for their kind permission to reproduce the photographs in this book:

1 Marijke Heuff (Patricia van Roosmalen); 2 Heather Angel; 3 Marijke Heuff (Mr & Mrs Jaap Nieuwenhuis and Paula Thies); 4 Eric Crichton (Turn End); 6–7 Philippe Perdereau; 8–9 Georges Lévèque; 10 above Jerry Harpur (Herterton House); 10 below Tania Midgley; 10–11 Marijke Heuff (Ineke Greve); 12–13 Philippe Perdereau; 14 Gary Rogers; 15 Eric Crichton; 16–17 above Tania Midgley; 16–17 below Gary Rogers; 17 Tania Midgley; 18–19 Georges Lévèque; 20 Lamontagne; 21 Philippe Perdereau; 22–23 Philippe Perdereau; 23 Andrew Lawson; 24 S & o Mathews; 25 Philippe Perdereau; 26–27 Philippe Perdereau; 28 Marijke Heuff (Mrs Goossenaerts); 29 Lamontagne; 30 above Eric Crichton (Crossing House); 30 above right Marijke Heuff (garden at Castle de Wiersse); 30 below Lamontagne; 31 Lamontagne; 32–33 Marijke Heuff (Mr F de Greeuw & Mr F Tiebout); 33 Eric Crichton (Mrs Dexter); 34–35 Georges Lévèque; 36–37 Andrew Lawson/Conran Octopus; 38 Marijke Heuff (Zaanse Schans); 39 above Marijke Heuff; 39 below left Gary Rogers; 39 below right Tania Midgley; 40 Andrew Lawson; 40–41 Andrew Lawson/Conran Octopus; 42–43 Jerry Harpur (Cambridge Botanic Garden); 43 above Jerry Harpur; 43 below Gary Rogers; 44 above left S & O Mathews; 44 above right Andrew Lawson; 44 below left Jerry Harpur; 44 below right Philippe Perdereau; 45 Jerry Harpur; 46–47 Marijke Heuff (Mr & Mrs Verstraten); 48–49 Andrew Lawson; 49 above Philippe Perdereau; 49 below Marijke Heuff (Ineke Greve); 50 above Marijke Heuff (designer Mien Ruys); 50 below Marijke Heuff (Little Lodge); 51 Gary Rogers; 52–53 Marijke Heuff (Barnsley House); 53 Marijke Heuff (Mr & Mrs Lambooy); 54–55 Philippe Perdereau; 56 Gary Rogers; 57 above Eric Crichton (The Old Rectory); 57 centre Andrew Lawson; 57 below Jerry Harpur (Mottisfont); 58 Linda Burgess/Insight; 58–59 Georges Lévèque; 60 Jill Marais/Garden Picture Library; 61 Andrew Lawson; 62 Philippe Perdereau; 63 Philippe Perdereau, below Eric Crichton; 64–65 Fritz von der Schulenburg; 66 Eric Crich-

ton; 66–67 Jerry Harpur (designer Tom Savery); 68 Jerry Harpur; 69 above Tania Midgley; 69 below Georges Lévèque; 70 Boys Syndication; 71 Heather Angel; 72–73 Georges Lévèque; 74 Philippe Perdereau; 75 Eric Crichton (Winslow Gardens); 76 above Philippe Perdereau; 76 below S & O Mathews; 76–77 Georges Lévèque; 78 Gary Rogers; 78–79 above Philippe Perdereau; 78–79 below S & O Mathews; 79 Andrew Lawson; 81 Jerry Harpur (Tyninghame); 82 Gary Rogers; 83 above Gary Rogers; 83 below Eric Crichton; 84 above Gary Rogers; 84 below left Tania Midgley; 84 below right Gary Rogers; 85–86 S & O Mathews; 87 Eric Crichton (Capel Manor); 88–89 Philippe Perdereau; 90 Marijke Heuff (designer Yak Ritzen); 90–91 above Marijke Heuff (Mr & Mrs Adriaanse); 90–91 below Marijke Heuff; 91 Marijke Heuff (designer Jorn Copijn); 92 above Gary Rogers; 92 below Tania Midgley; 93 Marijke Heuff (designer Els Proost); 94–95 Georges Lévèque; 95 above Marijke Heuff (designer Mien Ruys); 95 below Marijke Heuff (Mr & Mrs van der Upwich); 96–97 Philippe Perdereau; 98 left Eric Crichton; 98–99 Lamontagne; 99 above Marijke Heuff (Mrs N van Gennep); 99 below S & O Mathews; 100–101 Andrew Lawson; 102 above Marijke Heuff (Weeks Farm, Kent); 102 below Marijke Heuff (de Rhulenhof); 103 Philippe Perdereau; 104–105 Georges Lévèque; 105 Andrew Lawson; 106 Eric Crichton (Crossing House); 107 Georges Lévèque; 108–109 Georges Lévèque; 110 Gary Rogers; 111 above Tania Midgley; 111 below left Philippe Perdereau; 111 below right Marijke Heuff; 112–113 Andrew Lawson; 113 above Philippe Perdereau; 113 below Marijke Heuff (Mrs & Mrs Groenewegen); 114–115 Jerry Harpur (Herterton house); 115 above left S & O Mathews; 115 above right Georges Lévèque; 115 below Eric Crichton; 116–117 Gary Rogers; 117 Jerry Harpur (designer Thomasina Tarling); 118 Eric Crichton (Turn End); 118–119 Georges Lévèque; 120–121 Philippe Perdereau; 122 Fritz von der Schulenburg; 123 Ron Sutherland/Garden Picture Library (designer Michael Balston); 124–125 Andrew Lawson; 126–127 S & O Mathews; 127 above Andrew Lawson; 127 below Marijke Heuff (Ineke Greve); 128 Aldo Ballo; 129

Jerry Harpur (Garry van Egmond); 130–131 Georges Lévèque; 132 above Lamontagne; 132 below Marijke Heuff (Ineke Greve); 133 Lamontagne; 134 Andrew Lawson; 135 Gary Rogers; 137 Christine Tiberghien; 138 Gary Rogers; 138–139 Georges Lévèque; 140–141 Marijke Heuff (Hidcote); 141 above Marijke Heuff (designer Jacques Wirtz); 141 below Philippe Perdereau; 142 Gary Rogers; 143 above Marijke Heuff (Patricia van Roosmalen); 143 below Marijke Heuff (designer Jacques Wirtz); 144 Jerry Harpur (Tyninghame); 145 Georges Lévèque; 146–147 Georges Lévèque; 148 above Boys Syndication; 148 below Jerry Harpur (Jocelyn Ritchie); 148–149 Camera Press; 150 Georges Lévèque; 151 Agence Top/Robert Cesar; 152–153 Georges Lévèque; 154–155 Georges Lévèque; 156–157 Marijke Heuff (Mr F de Greeuw & Mr F Tiebout); 157 Eric Crichton (Long Hall); 158 above Andrew Lawson; 158 below Tania Midgley; 159 Andrew Lawson; 160 Eric Crichton (Broughton Castle); 161 Georges Lévèque; 162 Philippe Perdereau; 162–163 Gary Rogers; 164–165 Marijke Heuff (Jacques Wirtz); 166-167 Lamontagne; 168 above Philippe Perdereau; 168 below left Jay Patrick/Elizabeth Whiting & Associates; 168 below centre Christian Sarramon; 168 below right Ron Sutherland/Garden Picture Library; 169 Marijke Heuff (designer Piet Blanckaert); 170 above Jacqui Hurst/Boys Syndication; 170 below Eric Crichton (Hill Court); 170–171 Lamontagne; 172 Eric Crichton (The Old Rectory); 173 above Philippa Lewis/Edifice; 173 below Jerry Harpur (designer Thomasina Tarling); 174–175 Georges Lévèque; 176 S & O Mathews; 177 Marijke Heuff; 178 Philippe Perdereau; 179 above Gary Rogers; 179 below Jerry Harpur; 180 Andrew Lawson; 180–181 Marijke Heuff (Mrs M van Bennekom); 183 Jerry Harpur (designer Barbara Wenzel); 184–185 Marijke Heuff (Ineke Greve); 185 above Tessa Traeger; 185 below Gary Rogers; 186–187 Marijke Heuff (Mr & Mrs Poley); 187 Jerry Harpur/Conran Octopus (Terence and Caroline Conran); 188 left Ron Sutherland/Garden Picture Library (designer Murray Collins); 188 right Eric Crichton (Turn End); 189 Eric Crichton (Brook Cottage).